MW00531861

GO TO
HELL

WORDS OF WARNING

"If you are going THROUGH HELL,
keep going."
—WINSTON CHURCHILL

"The GATES OF HELL are open night
and day; / Smooth the descent, and easy is
the way: / But to return, and view the cheerful skies, /
In this the task and mighty labor lies ..."
—VIRGIL, *AENEID*

"Go to heaven for the climate,
HELL FOR THE COMPANY."
—MARK TWAIN

"HELL IS EMPTY
and all the devils are here."
—WILLIAM SHAKESPEARE

"The SAFEST ROAD TO HELL is the
gradual one—the gentle slope, soft underfoot,
without sudden turnings, without milestones,
without signposts."
—C. S. LEWIS

"ABANDON ALL HOPE,
ye who enter here."
—DANTE ALIGHIERI, *DIVINE COMEDY*

"HELL IS other people."
—JEAN-PAUL SARTRE

"HELL ISN'T other people.
HELL IS yourself."
—LUDWIG WITTGENSTEIN

"Long is the way and hard, that
OUT OF HELL leads up to light."
—JOHN MILTON, *PARADISE LOST*

"WHAT IS HELL? I maintain that it is
the suffering of being unable to love."
—FYODOR DOSTOEVSKY, *THE BROTHERS KARAMAZOV*

"We are each our own devil,
and we make this WORLD OUR HELL."
—OSCAR WILDE

"Maybe this world is
ANOTHER PLANET'S HELL."
—ALDOUS HUXLEY

"I hold it to be the inalienable right of
anybody to GO TO HELL in his own way."
—ROBERT FROST

Ethiopia's Afar region is home to
both the cradle of humankind
and a fiery lake of lava, spurring
some to call it the "Hellhole of
Creation."

GO TO HELL

A TRAVELER'S GUIDE TO EARTH'S MOST OTHERWORLDLY DESTINATIONS

ERIKA ENGELHAUPT

NATIONAL GEOGRAPHIC

Washington, D.C.

Since 1888, the National Geographic Society has funded more than 14,000 research, conservation, education, and storytelling projects around the world. National Geographic Partners distributes a portion of the funds it receives from your purchase to National Geographic Society to support programs including the conservation of animals and their habitats.

National Geographic Partners, LLC
1145 17th Street NW
Washington, DC 20036-4688 USA

Get closer to National Geographic Explorers and photographers, and connect with our global community. Join us today at nationalgeographic.org/joinus

For rights or permissions inquiries, please contact National Geographic Books Subsidiary Rights: bookrights@natgeo.com

Copyright © 2024 National Geographic Partners, LLC. All rights reserved. Reproduction of the whole or any part of the contents without written permission from the publisher is prohibited.

NATIONAL GEOGRAPHIC and Yellow Border Design are trademarks of the National Geographic Society, used under license.

Library of Congress Cataloging-in-Publication Data
Names: Engelhaupt, Erika, author.
Title: Go to Hell : a traveler's guide to Earth's most otherworldly
    destinations / Erika Engelhaupt.
Description: Washington, D.C. : National Geographic, 2024. | Includes
    index. | Summary: "This book features curated destinations across three
    hellish themes"-- Provided by publisher.
Identifiers: LCCN 2023046882 (print) | LCCN 2023046883 (ebook) | ISBN
    9781426223532 (hardcover) | ISBN 9781426223785 (ebook)
Subjects: LCSH: Voyages and travels. | Hell.
Classification: LCC G465 .E528 2024 (print) | LCC G465 (ebook) | DDC
    910.4--dc23/eng/20231122
LC record available at https://lccn.loc.gov/2023046882
LC ebook record available at https://lccn.loc.gov/2023046883

Printed in the United States of America

24/WOR/1

For Jay,
who has gone with me
to hell and back

CONTENTS

PART THREE
OTHERWORLDLY DESTINATIONS 200

Welcome to Hell

This is a book about the most hellish places on Earth—in a good way. I add that last bit because when I tell people that I'm writing about hellish places, they tend to squint, tilt their head, and say something like, "Like Phoenix?" Or, if they're New Yorkers: "Like New Jersey?" And then I say no, I'm not talking about hell*holes*—and for the record, I think both Phoenix and New Jersey have their selling points—but places that have some connection to the underworld as imagined by people and cultures throughout history.

This book is filled not with places you wouldn't want to go, but with hells that, I hope, you will soon want to see for yourself.

So, yes, this is a travel book about going to hell. And I can see why that might sound like an oxymoron. Perhaps you assume the point of traveling is to experience something as close to heaven on Earth as possible—say, gazing at azure waters while reclining on a cloud of fluffy white pillows. That certainly sounds like a lovely vacation. At least for a couple of hours, and then the pillows start to go a bit flat, you find yourself shifting around uncomfortably, and all that endless blue is a tad monotonous, no?

Caves and underground passages are often imagined to be gates to hell—
especially when they look as creepy as the caverns at England's Hodge Close Quarry.

Before you know it, you're trying to remember if you left the oven on, or whether the hotel has a bar. Because let's face it: Heaven can get a little boring. A book of the world's most heavenly places runs the same risk as a bottomless bowl of whipped cream: perfectly nice, but after the first couple bites, you've pretty much got the idea.

Hell, on the other hand, presents itself in endless varieties—and they'll keep you on your toes. You might find yourself peeking over the edge of a crater into a lake of fire (page 103), climbing through dark caverns in search of Hades (page 34), or hiking through an otherworldly expanse of volcanic landscape (page 226). Or you could explore lore involving castles, ghosts, monsters, evildoers, heroes, spirits, or gods. You might even find the world around you glowing, boiling, steaming, glittering, or flaming.

So if any of that piques your interest, and you'd like to add a little spark and sizzle to your world travels—say, in the form of fire and brimstone—I have some ideas for you.

After all, some of Earth's most awe-inducing sights have inspired hellish lore. Dramatic mountains and volcanoes, gorges and caves have long been considered boundaries between the realms of earth, air, and water. These liminal spaces, these gaps between worlds, are just the kinds of hidden places that the imagination tends to populate with the supernatural. Wherever earth breathes fire, ground shakes, foul gases spew, or rivers and lakes disappear mysteriously, people have said that the gods of the underworld must be at work.

Some of these places can be dangerous, even scary, but many are also breathtakingly beautiful. Caves are full of sparkling wonders (and crystallized fossils), volcanoes are draped in glowing red—or blue—and froths of steam top colorful pools of water. There are vast, stunning landscapes and small, intimate spaces where the faithful can contemplate the eternal.

A hell-themed world tour also provides a fascinating window into human history. People have always wondered what lies beyond life and death, and every culture and religion has formulated its own answers to this ultimate question. Seeing the similarities and differences in our versions of the afterlife tells us a lot about how human culture has spread across the globe and adapted to the different environments and phenomena that people encountered.

Mythology or Religion

Is hell a mythological place, or a religious one? In a sense, it's both.

People often use the word "myth" to mean something that's not true—like when scientists aim to "dispel a myth" about something—so it's easy to see why the word can easily offend. But in its broadest sense, the word "myth" just means a story or narrative—regardless of whether or not the story is based in historical fact.

Likewise, mythology is the body of traditional stories passed from generation to generation within a culture. These are our most important stories: They tell us about our origins, they explain the world and natural phenomena, and they recount important events in our history. They can be based in fact entirely, partly, or not at all—in any case, they're still myths. A religion, on the other hand, is a worldview that includes a mythology but also usually involves a set of shared beliefs, ritual practices, and moral teachings.

In this book, when I refer to mythology, it's in the sense of culturally important stories. We all have different stories about hell—where it is, who goes there, and what happens once they do. Referring to these stories as mythologies is not meant to imply anything about whose version of hell is right or wrong.

For instance, the seafaring people who populated the Pacific islands started in Taiwan and, over thousands of years, sailed throughout the Philippines and on to Papua New Guinea, Hawaii, and finally New Zealand. They brought ideas about the afterlife with them. So today, several Polynesian islands have a place at their northwestern tip considered a jumping-off point for spirits to plunge into the ocean and ultimately enter the afterlife. The details of the journey vary from island to island, but the roots of the idea are the same.

So what makes a place hellish enough to be included in this book? Well, I had a few criteria. First, locations had to have a physical feature of either natural or cultural importance, because this is, at its heart, a

Some places embrace the idea of being a hell on Earth, like the small outpost named Hell on Grand Cayman.

book about places. Second, they needed a connection to someone's vision of an underworld. It doesn't have to be Christian hell with flames and pits—though plenty of caves and volcanoes meet those criteria—but rather something that fits into at least one culture's idea of the afterlife or hidden realm. For instance, the Norse underworld Niflheim was described as an icy, misty place, and in Tibetan Buddhist tradition, there are eight primary hells (some of which are hot or fiery) but also eight cold hells, including a hell of chattering teeth.

And finally, all the stops on this world tour must have something amazing or fascinating to see. In other words, they're not entirely awful, but rather awesomely awful. They'll make you, sinner or not, want to get a glimpse of hell. Most of the places in this book are accessible to tourists, with many easy jaunts and some that are more of an adventure. I've included only a few places that are truly inaccessible, like the Cave of the Crystals in Mexico (page 206), because, well, they are so amazing and hellish that you need to see them, at least in these pages.

One thing this book is not: a guide to dark tourism, which tends to focus on places where something horrible once happened to someone, usually at the hands of other people. You won't find entries here about Auschwitz or war zones, or other places that are entirely man-made hells on Earth. (I have, however, included a couple of particularly interesting and hellish natural disasters, like the ancient city of Pompeii [page 155] that was destroyed by a volcanic eruption.)

Once I whittled down my list of possibilities, I found that my hellish places fit into three categories. Among the more than 50 places included, you'll find three kinds of hells: legendary portals to the underworld, natural wonders that inspire the word "hellscape," and otherworldly places that seem right out of a dark fairy tale.

The first chapter is "Portals to the Underworld." These are places that have a connection to hell according to a culture's myths, legends, or spiritual and religious beliefs. Often, these places have boundaries that blur between our world and the underworld (or whatever lies beyond the physical world). For instance, the ancient Greeks and their Roman successors were very influential in developing the idea of Hades, the pre-Christian hell of Western civilization. A number of ancient sites throughout those former empires were once seen as entrances to Hades.

The second chapter is "Hells on Earth." These are places that inspire our visions of hell. People on every continent and throughout human history have witnessed natural wonders like volcanoes erupting, burning pits, and steaming fissures in the earth. The result: They incorporated these phenomena into their concepts of hell or the underworld. Alternatively, some of the destinations in this chapter have been purposefully chosen to associate themselves with hell—like Hell, Michigan, which plays up its name with all kinds of devilish kitsch (page 130).

And the third and final chapter is "Otherworldly Destinations." These locations remind us of the underworld because they're dangerous, deadly, or in some cases just downright eerie. Some are home to creatures associated with hell, like bats or serpents, whereas others push visitors to the limits with their deadly features, from boiling rivers to flaming volcanoes. Either way, they draw adventurous travelers with the lure of danger, excitement, and one-of-a-kind sights.

I hope each of the hellscapes in this book will make you want to explore the world in a new way. You'll start to see surprising connections among people across the globe. We share the same kinds of hopes and dreams and fears about what lies beyond the world of the living, and our mythologies and legends about this other world tie us together.

In the end, there are plenty of ways to go to hell—but some are more fun than others. So let's get going.

A Very Brief History of Hell

Throughout human history, people have grappled with what comes after death. Different cultures and religions have their own answers to that question, but one thread across them all has remained surprisingly consistent: the ideas of heaven and hell. We see it in our oldest mythologies from around the world and in today's religions, too.

Take the *Epic of Gilgamesh,* for example. This tale of a semidivine Mesopotamian superhero is one of the oldest recorded stories in the world, first written in cuneiform on clay tablets as early as 2100 B.C. In it, the hero Gilgamesh goes on a quest for immortality and along the way journeys through an underworld to find the one man who can help him. There's a dark tunnel, a beastly guardian (in this case, half man, half scorpion), and a boatman who ferries our hero through the Waters of Death. Many of the same basic features crop up in later versions of hell, including Dante's *Inferno,* which plays an outsize role in the modern Western version of hell.

Meanwhile, ancient Egyptian scholars were writing their own account of the afterlife in the Book of the Dead, which was recorded in hieroglyphics carved inside pyramids and into coffins. The book spoke of three realms: heaven, earth, and an underworld known as Duat. This was a shadowy place of fear and peril that the dead were forced to navigate to reach the realm of heaven, known as the Field of Rushes. One crucial step in this journey was a judgment by the god Osiris. The god's jackal-headed son Anubis would place a soul's heart onto a scale, and if the heart was heavier with wickedness and sin than a feather, the soul would fail the test. No Field of Rushes for you: The monstrous Ammit, "eater of the dead," would end you forever.

The ancient Greeks had a similarly gloomy view of the underworld; theirs was a dark realm known as Hades. This was the Hades that Homer described in the epic poems *Odyssey* and *Iliad* around the eighth century B.C. In Homer's underworld, the vast majority of souls end up wandering as shades in Hades, and only the gods and semidivine merit either immortality in the heaven of the Elysian Fields, or endless torture like Sisyphus, forever pushing a boulder uphill. It was an eternal limbo devoid of joy or pleasure, where shades feel nothing and exist in a kind of dull twilight of semiconsciousness. About the only good thing you could say about Hades is that the Greeks, inventors of democracy, made even their afterlife democratic: All mortals—good or bad—ended up in the same place.

Over time, those who followed in the footsteps of the ancient Greeks elaborated on Hades, transforming it from a boring void to a place of judgment, like Duat, where the good and the bad were separated, and rewards and punishments meted out. At this point, hell starts to really get, well, hellish.

We see this shift among the Romans, who renamed the gods of the ancient Greeks and reinterpreted their myths. The most famous Roman version of Hades was that of Virgil (70 to 19 B.C.) in the *Aeneid,* which told the story of the hero Aeneas's journey to the underworld some seven

For the ancient Irish, the veil between our world and the spiritual Otherworld was thinnest on Samhain, a festival day still celebrated as Halloween.

centuries after Homer. In Virgil's telling, at a fork in the road through the underworld, to the right lies the path to a heavenlike place called Elysian Fields, and to the left lies the road to Tartarus, where sinners are punished for their mortal crimes. The oracle guiding Aeneas describes the tortures awaiting those who fail to make amends for their sins before death:

> No, not if I had a hundred tongues and a hundred mouths,
> and a voice of iron too—I could never capture
> all the crimes or run through all the torments,
> doom by doom.

Meanwhile, other versions of hell were flourishing around the world in the centuries both before and after the time of Christ. In Old Norse mythology, the goddess Hel is sent to rule the underworld of Niflheim, a cold and dreary purgatory where you'd find Vikings who were not fortunate enough to die in glorious battle and go to Valhalla, the Viking heaven. The Norse goddess's name would take root in the Old English word *helan,* and eventually "hell."

In East Africa, Swahili animist belief combined with Muslim thought to describe a hell called *kuzimu,* in which an elaborate maze reached deep below the earth, descending through seven levels with the worst sinners at the bottom, stuck in an icy cold eternity. The Aztec, too, had a forbidding hell called Mictlan, and the Maya described a nine-level underworld known as Xibalba. In Asia, both Buddhist and Hindu teachings included a realm of hell called Naraka, where sinners are tormented after death.

So by the time Christianity began to spread, much of the world was already pretty familiar with the idea of hell. Christians, however, certainly popularized their notion of it as a place of torment for the wicked.

Medieval Christians were particularly taken with elaborate hells; when Dante Alighieri wrote his three-part epic poem *Divine Comedy* in the 14th century, he gave hell nine levels, or circles, containing different kinds of sinners with devilishly appropriate punishments for each (see Dante's *Inferno,* page 153).

Today, religious scholars debate whether hell should be considered a literal place of punishment or more of a metaphor for the state of unending separation from God that awaits nonbelievers. Ideas vary even among Christians: Catholic doctrine rejects a literal hell but accepts purgatory for the purification of souls before heaven, while some other denominations take a more fire-and-brimstone approach.

Yet overall, hell remains pretty popular. The majority of Americans say they believe in both heaven and hell (though hell's numbers have slipped a bit in recent decades). A 2021 poll by the Pew Research Center found that 73 percent of U.S. adults say they believe in heaven, while 62 percent believe in hell. And hell remains a fixture in art and entertainment with shows like *Forever, The Good Place, Lucifer,* and *Good Omens* offering up modern visions of the afterlife (which involve, respectively, eternities of mid-century modern suburbs, frozen yogurt, guilt, and paperwork).

All in all, we seem to be just about as obsessed with hell and hellscapes as ever. Maybe hell is so satisfying because it gives us an outlet to imagine all the punishments we think wrongdoers deserve. Or because heaven, which by its nature is always pleasant, is just a little dull. Whatever the reason, and whether or not we believe in it literally, it seems to be in human nature to be curious about the "down below."

PART ONE

PORTALS
— TO THE —
UNDERWORLD

People throughout history have spoken of the underworld as a place where the dead reside—though some cultures claim the underworld, or otherworld, hosts different inhabitants. In some tales, it's filled with spirits and mystical beings, the home of gods and goddesses, ghosts, fairies, demons, devils, or monsters. Often the underworld is gloomy and dark, but sometimes it's a place of peace and light.

One thing is consistent across all human cultures: This other world exists in a spiritual realm that we can't see in our day-to-day lives. It lies "beyond."

But often, a hidden or secret door, a portal, or a gate leads into the underworld—just out of reach. These doors connect the living to the dead, or the mortal to the immortal. They offer the tantalizing possibility of stepping into the beyond. And who wouldn't want to get a peek through that keyhole? Imagine glimpsing red-hot lakes of fire, or the final river a soul must cross, or the realm of underworld gods.

Cultures around the world have developed vivid ideas about
what lies beyond the grave.

PAGE 22: Roelant Savery's "Orpheus in the Underworld" depicts the Greek hero's legendary journey into the land of the dead to rescue his wife, Eurydice.

In this section, I'll take you around the world to do just that. We'll visit locales that eons of mythology and lore have identified as gateways, portals, or "thin spots" in the veil of reality. These are places where two worlds collide, and where the living, the dead, and whatever other creatures reside in the underworld can meet.

Usually, the underworld is said to lie literally underground; hence, caves and pits serve as gateways of entry. For the ancient Greeks, the spike-encrusted caverns at Cape Matapan were a way to get to Hades (page 34). In Ireland, the Cave of the Cats, or Oweynagat, was the entrance to a supernatural realm (page 53). And Christians around the world have told stories of various gates to hell. One lies in a pit under an Irish monastery and leads to purgatory (page 65); a medieval castle in Czechia covers another (page 74).

One thing that many gates to hell and entrances to the underworld have in common is that they're found in the world's liminal spaces. These are the in-between places, the borderlands, where land meets sea, air meets earth, or above meets below. Along with caves, they include lakes, rivers, and mountaintops. They are places where one sits on the edge of another world.

Water is another important theme of these entrances. The ancient Maya, Greeks, and Romans all believed certain bodies of water served as boundaries between worlds. We'll go to some of the places that were most important in their ancient mythology, like the Acheron River (page 29), which a ferryman rowed across carrying dead souls to Hades in Homer's *Odyssey,* and the sinkholes, called cenotes, where the Maya entered their underworld, Xibalba (page 93).

Then there are the places of the dead, where souls of the departed linger, however briefly, before moving on. I'll take you along with me to Cape Reinga in New Zealand (page 89), where the spirits of Maori people are said to leap into the afterlife, and to New Orleans (page 107), where

The Geology of Hell

Cenotes, calderas, solfataras, and fumaroles: They all figure into hellish landscapes, but what are they? Here are definitions of some of the geological features you'll see in this book:

CALDERA: A type of crater that forms after a volcanic eruption, when the central part of a volcano is emptied of magma and collapses.

CENOTE: A natural reservoir of water found underground, often resulting from the collapse of limestone that exposes groundwater below.

CRATER: Any pit or depression created by an explosion or impact.

FUMAROLE: A hole in or near a volcano from which hot gas and steam are emitted.

GEOTHERMAL: Relating to heat generated in Earth's interior.

GEYSER: A spring that periodically erupts, ejecting a turbulent stream of hot water and steam. Geysers only occur near volcanic areas where magma heats water trapped by rock, causing pressure to build and create a hydrothermal explosion.

HOT SPRING: A natural spring producing warm water (usually defined as 70°F/21°C or higher) heated by geothermal activity beneath the surface.

MAGMA: Molten rock under Earth's crust. Once magma flows onto Earth's surface, it's called lava.

SOLFATARA: A volcanic area or vent that releases hot vapors and sulfurous gases. The word comes from the Latin *sulpha terra,* or "land of sulfur."

SUPERVOLCANO: A volcanic center that has had an eruption of the highest level, a magnitude 8 on the volcanic explosivity index, meaning that at some point it erupted more than 249 cubic miles (1,040 km³) of material. Eruptions this large create a caldera at the site of the ejected magma.

the dead (and occasionally the living) pass through the seven Gates of Guinee in the city's cemeteries. And we'll visit Japan's Mount Osore (page 85), where the families of children who have died are reunited with their spirits amid an otherworldly landscape.

These places are wildly different from one another, yet have a lot in common. For one, they show how many cultures around the world have richly imagined hellscapes as places of punishment. For all of our detailed explanations of hell and the underworld—from Dante's nine circles of hell to the bureaucratic labyrinth of Chinese hell, we all seem to love seeing bad guys get their comeuppance in the end. And more than that, we all seek to understand life and what comes after it. We come back to the same ideas over and over again: looking to nature for clues to the order of the universe, and seeking connections with our gods and the spirits of those we have lost.

In the end, I believe, our heavens and hells tie us together, and our special places unite us.

The Acheron

Take in the mystical beauty of a river to hell.

On the western coast of Greece, a crystal clear river runs to the Ionian Sea, flowing through picturesque mountains and majestic gorges as it winds through the Epirus region. It's so beautiful that it's hard to believe this is the famed River of Woe, the Acheron, cursed by the gods and leading to the mythic Greek underworld of Hades.

The Acheron, one of the most storied rivers in written history, is known as one of the five rivers running through Hades. Around the eighth century B.C., the river appeared in Homer's *Odyssey* as an entrance to Hades and the site of the Nekromanteion (a temple where a prophet, known as an oracle, would communicate with the dead). In another legend, the mythical Titans gained strength by drinking from the river, allowing them to defeat the Olympians for control of the universe. This angered the god Zeus so much that he cursed the Acheron, forcing the river underground and turning its waters dark and bitter.

Homer's description of the Acheron in the *Odyssey* marked the first time a physical river was linked to a mythical one from the underworld, giving people a real-world destination to possibly access Hades. At the time of the *Odyssey,* multiple rivers throughout the Mediterranean region were actually called Acheron, and more than one was claimed to be *the* Acheron of Homer. But the Acheron in the Epirus region of Greece is most consistently associated with the epic and the land of the dead.

Today, the Acheron still lures travelers with natural pools and waterfalls strung along the 32-mile-long (52 km) river amid charming villages steeped in Greek history. Visitors come to hike and swim, or float peacefully down it by canoe or kayak. To complete the dip into Greek mythology, check out a popular archaeological site along the river said to hold the remains of the Nekromanteion, the ancient temple housing the oracle of the dead. The temple was described in ancient writings as lying near the northwest shore of the Acherusian Lake, which formed where the Acheron flowed into the other four rivers of Hades (see page 32).

The ancient Greeks believed that the spirits of the dead entered the underworld at special places that led underground, such as the Nekromanteion, and that the living could sometimes communicate with the dead at these sites. Pilgrims would come to the Nekromanteion to attempt to speak to long-gone loved ones and to learn from them what the future would hold. According to lore, visitors would enter a dark chamber under the temple and perform rituals and ceremonies to prepare to commune with the dead.

In 1958, a team of archaeologists discovered the ruins of a building from the third or fourth century B.C. in the village of Mesopótamos that seemed to fit the descriptions of ancient lore: a thick-walled main building, subterranean chambers, and idols of the underworld goddess Persephone. So they announced they had found the Nekromanteion. Later research cast doubt on the site's purposes, suggesting it may have been

The Acheron Springs near Glyki, Greece, feed a river that ancient Greeks believed flowed into the underworld.

The Rivers of Hell

In the physical world, rivers mark borders and divide territories; in mythology, they often separate the underworld from the land of the living. Rivers carry water, the stuff of life, but many cultures also believe rivers are brimming with fire, or even blood.

Such is the case in Greek mythology, which speaks of five rivers that run through the underworld. Each had its own distinct nature and function and was associated with its own god, goddess, or emotion:

STYX: The name Styx refers to the most famous underworld river, the main river of Hades, and also to a goddess said to live in a grotto at the entrance to said underworld. The Styx is the only river to appear in the *Iliad,* Homer's earliest text. In later tales, it becomes the river that all spirits must cross after death, with the ferryman Charon shuttling souls across.

ACHERON: The river of misery or woe was the next river to appear in poetry, and in some stories replaced Styx as the river across which Charon carried the dead.

COCYTUS: Known as the "river of wailing," the Cocytus is a branch of the Styx that flows into the Acheron in Homer's *Odyssey.* Plato described the Cocytus as emptying into the pit of Tartarus, the lowest level of Hades. The souls of the dead the ferryman Charon would not carry into Hades were said to wander the shores of the Cocytus.

PHLEGETHON: Plato described the Phlegethon as a stream filled with fire that coils around the world and flows into the pits of Hades. Dante wrote of it as a river of hot blood that boils sinners who committed crimes of violence. In one myth, the god Phlegethon and the goddess Styx fall in love and are united when Hades allows their rivers to both run into his domain.

LETHE: The souls of the dead are said to drink from the River Lethe, aka the river of oblivion, to forget their earthly lives before entering the underworld.

PORTALS TO THE UNDERWORLD | 33

a house or fortification, with the underground chambers used for storing grain or water.

Nevertheless, the site remains officially designated as the Nekromanteion and continues to draw visitors seeking the mystical oracle of the dead. Visitors can see remnants of the exterior walls and an entrance to what may have been the temple complex, plus the main building with its arched underground hall and rooms where—if the legends are true—ancient Greeks would have looked for the spirits of the dead among the shadows of flickering lantern lights.

With its combination of natural beauty and fascinating history, the Epirus coast is becoming more popular as a tourism destination. Nature lovers and adventure travelers can take in the diverse wildlife on a hike, then float down the Acheron's blue waters while enjoying the enchanting scenery—and connecting with its eerie history.

In fact, so many people are flocking to the area that Greek officials are starting to worry about their impact on the river's ecosystem, which includes a number of rare or endangered plants and animals, including golden eagles and Egyptian vultures. So, please, go see the ancient river of Homer's Hades and imagine yourself on a day trip to the underworld—but remember to tread lightly along its shores.

Cape Matapan

Sail into the hellish site of a tragic Greek love story.

At the southernmost point of mainland Greece lies a small point of rocky, grass-covered land called the Mani Peninsula, and at the tip of that peninsula is Cape Matapan, also known as Cape Tainaron or Taenarum. Tucked into the cliffs on the cape is a cave, which ancient Greeks believed to be an entrance to the underworld, Hades.

In Greek mythology, Hades is the underworld kingdom located at the edge of the earth and ruled by a god of the same name. "The edge of the earth" was considered a place where land meets sea, or the underground. A cave, such as the one at Cape Matapan, is both and was a logical place to situate a gate to hell.

It also just looks right, with a ceiling bristling with spiky, appropriately menacing stalactites. Water has inundated the cave system, so the entrance, which leads into a network of caverns, now lies at sea level. Today, you need to take a tour by boat, but the view inside makes it worthwhile. As you float through the cave, it looks as if you're sailing under a ceiling of knives, making it easy to believe you're crossing the River Styx to enter the underworld.

According to Greek mythology, the horrible three-headed dog Cerberus guarded the cave at Cape Matapan to keep the dead from escaping

In ancient Greek tales, the hero Hercules performed 12 famous feats,
called labors, culminating in the capture of Cerberus, the doglike creature
that guarded the underworld, Hades.

Hades. The divine hero Heracles (Hercules to the Romans) entered the underworld through the cave at Cape Matapan and fought the beast, ultimately dragging him out of Hades.

The cave was also the setting of the ultimate Greek tragedy, the love story of Orpheus and Eurydice. To rescue his beloved from Hades, Orpheus negotiates with the gods Hades and Persephone to release her. The gods agree, on one condition: Orpheus must not gaze upon Euryd-

Ancient Greek Zombies

While you're touring the history of the underworld in Greece, another Greek nod to the dead—or undead—involves the ancient Greek origins of zombie mythology. At least 2,000 years ago, the ancient Greeks told stories of corpses that could reanimate, leaving their graves at night to harm the living. Today, you might see evidence of the steps Greeks took to prevent the dead from rising at ancient burial sites.

The risen undead, or revenants, were often believed to have been troublemakers or wicked people during their lifetime. In the second century, the Greek geographer Pausanias told a story of a rapist from Temesa who was stoned to death, only to return as a revenant to terrify villagers and demand the yearly sacrifice of a maiden to his violent urges.

To prevent suspected revenants from escaping the grave, the Greeks would sometimes pin down their corpses, or bury them on their stomachs or upside down to confuse their efforts to dig themselves from the ground. At the Kamarina necropolis in Sicily, for example, archaeologists found one skeleton buried with large vessels, called amphorae, covering its head and feet, and another covered by five large stones.

ice again until they both reach the light. As Orpheus exits the cave, he looks back in his excitement, only to see Eurydice vanish forever—she had not yet crossed into daylight.

Another piece of Greek history lies above the cave, more easily accessible on the cape. The city of Taenarum once stood atop Cape Matapan and was an important place of worship for the Spartans, who built several temples there. One was a temple to the sea god Poseidon that the Byzantines later converted into a church. If you visit today, you can see the ruins of Poseidon's temple on the hill above the caves, some of its stacked stone arches still intact.

⟨ BEFORE YOU GO

Cape Matapan is easy to reach by car or bike, with a road running to the tip of the peninsula and an old lighthouse on the point. Just north of the point is the Taenarum archaeological site with the ruins of the Temple of Poseidon. Beautiful swimming beaches are also tucked away along the peninsula, offering gorgeous views and solitude.

The cave entrance at Cape Matapan opens at sea level into a cliff face, so you'll need to charter a private boat to enter the caves, or you can view them from the shore. Alepotrypa, another reputed gateway to hell, is part of the Caves of Diros, about an hour's drive north of the tip of Cape Matapan. If you want to enter a cave, the Diros Caves are the easier bet, with available guided boat tours that go through the cave, which is also dripping with stalactites.

Pluto's Gate

This ancient gateway to the underworld still breathes deathly fumes.

I n 2013, Italian archaeologists announced a stunning discovery: a gate to hell. More precisely, they had unearthed the ruins of a Greco-Roman site known as Pluto's Gate, an infamous temple dedicated to the gods of the underworld.

Pluto's Gate, or the Ploutonion in Greek, was located in the ancient city of Hierapolis (modern-day Pamukkale, Turkey). The city was famous for its hot springs, which were believed to have healing powers, but its other popular attraction was the Ploutonion, a temple built at the mouth of a cave that exhaled deadly gases—so deadly, in fact, that the temple was dedicated to Pluto, the Roman god of death. Pluto, in turn, was based on the older Greek god Hades, who ruled over the underworld named for him.

Greek geographer Strabo described Pluto's Gate around 2,000 years ago: "This space is full of a vapor so misty and dense that one can scarcely see the ground. Any animal that passes inside meets instant death. I threw in sparrows and they immediately breathed their last and fell."

Some considered the gas to be a deadly exhalation from the gods of the underworld, or the foul breath of Cerberus (or Kerberos), the hell-hound guarding its gates. Today, we know the vapor was carbon dioxide emanating from the Babadag fault line beneath the cave, with levels that to this day are strong enough to kill birds that fly too close. Research published in 2019 put carbon dioxide levels anywhere from 4 to 53 percent at the mouth of the cave, and as high as 91 percent inside. Hardy Pfanz, a German volcanologist who studied the cave's gases, noted that levels of even 5 percent can start to affect mammals, and the concentrations found in parts of the cave could kill a person within a minute.

Toxicology aside, the mysterious killer cave seemed a likely candidate for an entrance to Hades, so the ancient Greeks built a temple on

A digital illustration reconstructs the ancient Ploutonion,
a sanctuary dedicated to the god Pluto (or Hades). An arched entrance
(bottom center) led into a toxic cave where animals were sacrificed.

top of the cavern dedicated to the underworld. Researchers found the remains of the site by tracing the underground source of gases that emerged at a hot spring where dead birds tended to accumulate. During the excavations, they found Ionic columns bearing inscriptions to the underworld gods Pluto and Kore (Hades and Persephone to the Greeks) as well as the remains of a temple, a pool, and steps that may have served as stadium seating for pilgrims, just as ancient writers had described.

Historically, pilgrims came from far and wide to worship and reach out to loved ones who had died—as well as to test out the cavern's deadly effects using small birds available for purchase on-site. Only priests, however, were believed able to enter the cave entrance. They would sacrifice larger animals, like bulls, by leading them into the cave and then dragging them out dead. Meanwhile, eunuch priests known as Galli would descend into the cave and return unharmed as evidence of their own divine protection. (Presumably, they survived by holding their breath and staying upright, because the gases settle toward the ground.)

Pilgrims were kept away from the cave by handrails but would often hang out as close as they could get, hoping to commune with the dead or receive a message from the underworld. Some would report visions and prophecies after spending time near the cave's entrance. This was likely the result of the gases' hallucinatory effect in small doses. (Archaeologists now think the famous Oracle of Delphi may have received her prophecies thanks to a seep of underground gases that caused hallucinations and a kind of ecstatic high.)

Today, visitors can see the excavated and partially rebuilt remains of the Ploutonion, including the stone gate built over the cave's entrance. A walkway running a safe distance from the gate allows a peek into this entrance to the underworld.

Cave of the Sibyl

Inside this eerie cavern, an oracle acted as gatekeeper to Hades.

There's a cliff at Cumae whose vast flank is cut
into a cave with a hundred shafts.
Through them rush the Sibyl's answers,
hundredfold.
—Virgil, *Aeneid*

t's one of the world's most famous entrances to hell. The Cave of the Sibyl (or Antro della Sibilla in Italian) was described 2,000 years ago as a gateway to the underworld with a hundred mouths and home to a terrifying oracle, a priestess who could predict the future.

Today, you enter this famous portal to Hades through a passageway of towering stones that lean inward, forming an open-topped arch that funnels you toward a foreboding trapezoidal hole in a steep hillside. As you enter the cool dampness of the cavern, it becomes apparent why it was said to have so many entrances; periodic openings along the long stone hallway cast light and shadows that give the illusion of repeating doors. It feels as if you're walking through a set of mirrors leading into the unknown.

You'll find the Cave of the Sibyl in Cumae (Cuma), a seaside town outside of Naples founded around the eighth century B.C. by the first Greek colonists to arrive on Italy's mainland. The settlers constructed a

temple to Apollo at the top of a hill and expanded an existing cave below as the workplace of their oracle, also known as a sibyl, a priestess who could commune with the gods to answer questions or make prophecies.

According to legend, the Sibyl of Cumae started out as a pretty and non-terrifying young woman named Amalthaea. Noticing her beauty, the sun god Apollo offered her one wish in exchange for her virginity. Amalthaea was a quick thinker, and she pointed to a pile of dirt and wished for a year of life for each particle it held. But she didn't think quickly enough, because she didn't ask to remain young for each of those years. Instead, she grew old but could not die. Thus, she fit the trope of the scary old lady. The writer Virgil described her as a crone scribbling prophecies on oak leaves scattered outside her cave; another famous legend depicts her as powerful, but conniving. In the story, the sibyl writes nine books prophesying the future of Rome. The king of Rome refuses to pay her exorbitant price for the books, so she begins burning them three at a time until, finally, the king relents and buys the last three. Known as the Sibylline Books, the writings laid out rituals to avert disaster and were stored in a vault under the Temple of Jupiter to be pulled out in times of crisis.

Throughout the Greek colonies, there were only 10 oracles—the most famous today is the Oracle of Delphi, but the sibyl of Cumae would have been the one best known to the ancient Romans. The oracles were no common fortune tellers; they communicated with the gods by entering a state of divine ecstasy—maybe after eating certain herbs, or inhaling toxic gases (see Pluto's Gate, page 38)—to deliver prophecies. For the ancient Greeks, consulting a sibyl was a big deal; the oracles wouldn't deliver prophecies for just anyone, and they were considered,

Openings that cast light into the Cave of the Sibyl, or Antro della Sibilla, may have inspired its description as a cave with "a hundred mouths."

frankly, pretty awful to deal with. The writer Heraclitus was the first to describe one: "The Sibyl, with frenzied mouth uttering things not to be laughed at, unadorned and unperfumed, yet reaches to a thousand years with her voice by aid of the god."

Over several centuries, the Greeks, and then the conquering Romans, expanded the sibyl's cave, giving the main tunnel a roughly trapezoidal shape and adding side galleries and cisterns for collecting water. But eventually, Christianity became the dominant religion of the region and many old Greek and Roman temples were destroyed, repurposed, or abandoned. The city was destroyed during an invasion in the early 1200s, and eventually the site of the old Temple of Apollo and the sibyl's cave fell into ruin and was forgotten.

Then in 1932, Amedeo Maiuri, the same archaeologist who led excavations at Pompeii, discovered underground passages near the ruins of the Temple of Apollo and announced he had found the long-lost Cave of the Sibyl. Though heavily debated, what is now officially called the Antro della Sibilla is widely considered to be the likely site of the Oracle of Cumae.

The excavated cave at Cumae now consists of a 430-foot-long (131 m) tunnel, its stone walls carved into a tall, narrow passageway. Modern lighting along the tunnel's length emphasizes the chiaroscuro effect, in which bands of light and darkness create the famous illusion of many doors. At the back of the tunnel lies the room from which the sibyl would have made her pronouncements. Try out your best booming voice from that spot; it can be heard throughout the passageway— making it easy to imagine the terror that would have befallen those who came to hear the words of the great sibyl of Cumae.

The Roman writer Virgil memorialized this frightening sibyl in one of the most famous accounts of the underworld. In the *Aeneid,* the hero named Aeneas, who escaped the fall of Troy and went on to found Rome, comes to Cumae to ask the sibyl his future. From deep inside the cave with a hundred openings emerges the terrible voice of the sibyl. She predicts that Aeneas will prevail in his quest, then agrees to lead him into the underworld to see his dead father—with a warning that would become one of Virgil's most famous passages:

> Easy is the descent to Avernus [hell],
> for the door to the underworld lies open both day and night.
> But to retrace your steps and return to the breezes above—
> that's the task, that's the toil.

The sibyl then leads Aeneas into Hades, which Virgil placed beneath the nearby Lake Avernus (see page 46). The ferryman Charon carries them across the Acheron River (see page 29) into the land of the dead, who wander the gloom as shades—mere shadows of their former selves. Eventually the path splits, with the way to the right leading to the heavenly Elysium, and the left leading to Tartarus, where the wicked were punished. This, Virgil's vision of the afterlife, helped shape our ideas of heaven and hell today.

♆ BEFORE YOU GO

The Antro della Sibilla is part of the Cumae Archaeological Park (Parco Archeologico di Cuma), which houses the remnants of the ancient city of Cumae, the oldest Greek colony in Italy. Here you can see the ruins and excavated remains of the city's acropolis, or fortified hilltop, including the Temples of Apollo and Jupiter as well as a Roman crypt, thermal baths, and an amphitheater. Some of the explanatory signs are in disrepair or written only in Italian, so it's best to go with a guide who can explain what you're seeing and the history of the site.

Lake Avernus

Walk the shores of a dark portal to the underworld.

> There was a deep stony cave, huge and gaping wide,
> sheltered by a dark lake and shadowy woods,
> over which nothing could extend its wings in safe flight.
> —Virgil, *Aeneid*

These days, Lake Avernus (Lago d'Averno in Italian) is a peaceful vacation spot. Steep green slopes covered in vineyards and orange trees encircle the lake's cool, deep waters. There's a playground, restaurants full of chatting diners enjoying lunch alfresco, and even a lakeside wedding venue. But look a little closer—you'll notice how dark the waters are, and you may detect a slight odor of sulfur in the air. That's your first clue that something is a bit sinister in this lovely spot near the sea.

In ancient times, as the legends go, this lake was way creepier. Back then, dark cypress woods covered the hills and greater volcanic activity caused the lake to emit toxic fumes and a strong smell of rotten eggs. Though ducks paddle peacefully along its shores today, the lake got its

Lake Avernus's maximum depth is 200 feet (60 m).

name from the Greek *aornos,* meaning "without birds," as it was said that birds could not fly over Lake Avernus without falling dead from the sky.

The lake sits in an extinct volcanic crater near the Phlegraean Fields, a landscape shaped by volcanoes and also known as Campi Flegrei, or the "burning fields." The underlying volcanic soil gives the lake its dark color, which ranges from a deep blue to a foreboding charcoal gray depending on the light. The waters are deep, reaching more than 200 feet (60 m), and the hills rising around the lakeshore create the feeling of being trapped inside a bowl. It's easy to see how Lake Avernus could be seen as a portal to somewhere, and probably no place good.

The ancient Greeks saw the deep waters as a link to the mythical underground River Styx, which carried the dead to Hades. Likewise, the Romans considered the lake to be the entrance to the underworld, and some Roman writers sometimes even used its name as another term for Hades. Most famously, the Roman poet Virgil moved the entrance of hell from Greece to his home turf, sending his hero Aeneas to the underworld through an oracle's cave on the shore of Lake Avernus in the *Aeneid.*

The Romans built villas on the shores of Lake Avernus, despite its connection to hell. Eventually, the lakeside became an accessible getaway for the wealthy, who would lounge in a series of thermal baths until sunset. The stone remains of one of the bathhouses can still be seen on the lakeshore today, right next to the public walking path.

Nearby, you can also visit another spot once rumored to be an entrance to Hades. Look for a sign pointing to the Grotta della Sibilla next to a narrow, wooded trail. This unassuming dirt path leads to a rusty metal grate covering the entrance to a cavern in the hillside. Peek inside, and a small pile of trash is all that now covers the rock floor. This spot was once thought to be the Cave of the Sibyl, where Virgil wrote that the female prophet guided Aeneas into Hades. However, the cave was misidentified. The cavern, it turns out, is not Greek (it's arched, a Roman construction) and was most likely a Roman military tunnel built to carry supplies to the other side of the hill. Instead, the real Cave of the Sibyl is now believed to be a few miles away in the Cumae Archaeological Park (see page 45).

Despite the litter, the mystery and legends associated with Lake Avernus and its grotto make it a worthwhile stop on a tour of the region's many hell-themed destinations. Walk around the lake and perhaps stop to read a bit from Virgil and imagine his hero's journey to the underworld.

Lacus Curtius

Rome's gateway to hell is hidden in plain sight—at one of its biggest tourist destinations.

Most of the millions of tourists who visit the famed Roman Forum each year walk right past a patio-size paved area holding a circle of stones in the heart of the plaza, never realizing they're passing over an ancient gateway to hell.

For centuries, the Forum was at the center of daily life for Romans. Built piecemeal over many centuries on land that had once been a marshy lake, it was a hub of social and political activity—a marketplace, government center, and gladiatorial arena all in one. The Cloaca Maxima, one of the world's first sewers, drained most of the marsh. But one spot in the middle of the Forum never fully emptied; instead, it became a pond that eventually shrank to just a small basin.

The pit, of course, spawned various legends about its origins. One of the most famous is the tale of Marcus Curtius. As the story goes, a mysterious chasm opened up in the center of the Forum at some point early in its history. The pit was endless and could not be filled with dirt, though the Romans tried. So they consulted an oracle, who told the people that to close the chasm they must sacrifice the things that made them great. If they did, Rome would live forever. Upon hearing the prophecy, a brave young soldier named Marcus Curtius armed himself, mounted his horse, and plunged into the chasm, sacrificing himself for the greater good of Rome. The chasm closed upon him, Rome was saved, and the spot in the middle of the Forum was named for him and his valor.

The Romans continued to treat the Lacus Curtius as a holy site through the centuries. Some believed it to be an entrance to Hades, and Marcus Curtius's life to be an offering to the god of the underworld. During the time of Augustus Caesar, it's said that every Roman would throw a coin into the Lacus Curtius as a blessing for the emperor's well-being—an offering to the gods down below.

According to legend, Marcus Curtius saved Rome by leaping on his steed into the Lacus Curtius, an entrance to the underworld in the city's Forum.

Today, the Lacus Curtius is an unassuming stack of stone in the Forum's ruins, near the more impressive fluted marble Column of Phocas. A small area is paved with stone and, under a metal awning, a roughly circular arrangement of stones marks the Lacus Curtius pit itself. At the edge of the site stands a copy of a bas-relief carving of Marcus Curtius, unearthed from the Forum centuries ago, showing the soldier with shield and spear at his side, ready to ride his steed into the underworld.

Oweynagat Cave

A passageway to the Irish "Otherworld" is now a gateway to hell.

Frightful things are said to fly out of a certain small, dark cave in Ireland. Often referred to as "Ireland's hell cave," the cave's story is far older than today's Christian notion of hell—in fact, it's older than Christianity itself. This wee crack in the earth is at the center of thousands of years' worth of legends and myth, including the origins of the Samhain festival, the forebearer to today's Halloween.

Over thousands of years, the cave has borne many names. It's been called Síd Crúachan, or the Otherworldly Mound of Crúachan. Many today know it as Oweynagat, or the Cave of the Cats, a reference to a mythological tale of warriors trapped in the cave overnight with three magical wildcats. But when Christians started recording traditional Irish tales in the 12th century, they heard of the cave's connection to a world beyond the mortal plain and began to describe it as *dorus iffiirn na Hérend*, or "Ireland's gate to hell."

Oweynagat cave is located in Roscommon, a rural county in the north-central part of the country. This is a land of sprawling farms, where sheep graze on rolling hills and roads are narrow, twisty, and lined with thick hedges. It's part of a sprawling site called Rathcroghan, which means "Fort of Crúachan." Crúachan was the sacred capital of

Connacht, one of five ancient kingdoms of Ireland. Rathcroghan was an important ceremonial and burial site where kings were crowned, judgments were passed, and great festivals were held. These days, Rathcroghan is a collection of 240 archaeological sites spanning more than 5,000 years of history and spread across two and a half square miles (6.5 km²).

The entrance to the "hell cave" itself is unassuming: a small, roughly triangular hole in the ground, mostly hidden by a hedge in a corner of a farmer's field. To enter, you have to crouch down and drop your feet onto a ledge, then duck low while shimmying through an opening just big enough for an adult to pass. Next you duck to the left and carefully pick your way down a rocky incline until, finally, the passageway opens up. You find yourself standing in a rift in the rock, tall and sharply pointed at the top, that stretches back 120 feet (37 m). There are no signs on the walls of soot or anything that once held a light; those who entered the cave in ancient times would have done so in pitch blackness. In the cool, damp darkness, it's easy to see why the cave would have seemed another world.

Heading back aboveground, you pass through a series of stones, called lintels, that were stacked and braced during the Early Medieval period to construct an entryway. Above the entrance, as you look out, you'll see a large flat stone carved with a series of lines. They look almost like tally marks one might make to count off the passage of days, but this is actually writing—an ogham inscription, the earliest form of Irish writing, dating back to between the fourth and eighth centuries A.D. The inscription translates to "[the stone of] Fráoch, son of Medb." It is believed to be the earliest written reference in Ireland to Queen Medb

The cave known as Oweynagat, or Cave of the Cats, was thought to be a portal to the Otherworld, a magical ancient Irish underworld.

(or Maeve), the Iron Age warrior queen. Maeve is now seen as a purely mythological figure, but tales of her adventures have captivated the Irish people for so long that many assume she was a real ruler of ancient Connacht.

To the pagans of ancient Ireland, this cave was sacred, as both a door to the Otherworld and a place where young warriors would test their courage. It also played an important role in the pagan festival known as Samhain, which celebrated the end of the harvest and the coming of winter each October 31. As nights grew longer and a chill filled the air, Samhain marked not only the transition of seasons but also transitions between worlds. It is said that on October 31, the borders to the Otherworld fall open, allowing spirits to cross over—especially via Oweynagat, where the border between the worlds is thinnest.

The cave was also said to be the home of the frightful Morrígan, a shape-shifting Otherworld goddess who often takes the form of a crow. On Samhain, she would fly from the cave and spread mayhem far and wide. She had help in the form of a swarm of three-headed beasts called Aillén Tréchenn, birds whose breath would wither the leaves off trees, and a horde of magical wild pigs whose numbers multiplied when anyone tried to count them. Together, these creatures would prepare the land for winter—but you wouldn't want to cross paths with them, lest you are dragged back into the Otherworld. So began the tradition of disguising oneself as one of them on Samhain night, to avoid being taken. Sound familiar?

The Christian mystics who followed St. Patrick to Ireland tried to stamp out pagan rituals like Samhain. Failing to eliminate them, they instead rebranded them. Samhain eventually became Halloween, and the cave of Oweynagat became a portal to hell. But the Otherworld of the Irish, also known as Tír na nÓg, was nothing like the Christian hell; for one thing, you didn't need to die to go there. Instead, it was a different realm with links to our physical world. Certain places allowed easier access to the Otherworld, especially in-between places such as bogs, lakes, and caves, like Oweynagat, where the worlds above and below join.

The ancient Otherworld was also a place of both good and evil. It was a world of gods, and of supernatural beings known as Sídh or Sí (pronounced "shee"). The Sí and other otherworldly supernatural beings, called Tuatha Dé Danann, are often referred to now as fairies, which may conjure up images of cute little waifs with wings. But these were no trifling pixies; rather they were powerful beings with complicated relationships to mortals. When a mortal entered their realm,

How to Say It

The pronunciation of Irish words is notoriously difficult. Here's a guide to help you travel and tour Ireland's hell-related places:

RATHCROGHAN: Rath-crah-un

OWEYNAGAT: Owen-na-gat

CONNACHT: Con-noct

CRÚACHAN: Crew-ah-can

SAMHAIN: Sow-en

SÍDH: Shee

TÍR NA NÓG: Teer-na-nowg

MEDB: May-v

LOUGH: Lok

they would discover a beautiful land where time and seasons were suspended—hardly the fiery hell that Christians imagined.

Yet the name stuck. Oweynagat was first recorded as *dorus iffiirn na Hérend,* or Ireland's gate to hell, in the 12th century in a medieval Irish manuscript called the *Lebor Laignech,* based on a story dating back to the ninth century in which the magical pigs and three-headed creatures of Samhain are recast as beasts of hell. After all, the Otherworld did have its dark side—so the cave took on a new kind of symbolism, as a passage to a demon-filled underworld.

Today, you can journey into the cave that inspired these legends. The week of Halloween is an excellent time to visit and take in a special tour highlighting the origins of Samhain. Then on Halloween night, make your way an hour and a half east to the Hill of Ward in County Meath (see page 59), where modern pagan worshippers gather for their main Samhain celebration and lighting of ceremonial fires.

♆ BEFORE YOU GO

Oweynagat cave is on private land and can be entered only with a guide from the Rathcroghan Visitor Centre. Tours of the Rathcroghan archaeological sites and the cave can be scheduled online for a fee. To preserve the cave, self-exploration is strictly forbidden. Reservations are required, and tour groups are limited to nine visitors, so make sure to plan ahead.

Hill of Ward and Hill of Tara

The ancient roots of Halloween are found in the Irish countryside.

t's said that on a clear day, you can see half of Ireland from the top of the Hill of Tara. Its long ridge drops steeply to the west, offering dramatic views of endless Irish green. This idyllic spot has been Ireland's most sacred land for the past 5,000 years and lies at the heart of many ancient myths and legends. The hill is home to the Stone of Destiny that chose kings, a tomb with mysterious links to the origins of Halloween, and an entrance to the Irish Otherworld, home of gods and mythical beings.

Located outside the town of Navan in County Meath, the Hill of Tara is less than an hour's drive from Dublin, but it couldn't feel farther from the bustling, modern city. Centuries ago, the hill was covered and surrounded by so many monuments, earthworks, burial mounds, and natural features of spiritual importance, such as springs and streams, that around A.D. 1000 an Irish court poet wrote "Dindgnai Temrach"—or "The Remarkable Places of Tara"—to document them all. One of them was a ritual stone pillar called the Lia Fáil or Stone of Destiny, which according to Irish mythology was carried to Tara by

the gods and would let out a mighty roar when touched by the rightful king of the land.

Another remarkable place on Tara is a passage tomb inside a hillock known as the Mound of the Hostages, which got its name during the medieval period when warring factions would trade hostages there. But the tomb inside is much, much older; it was built around 3000 B.C. and was used as a Neolithic burial place for at least 1,500 years. The tomb is a small stone-lined passageway that's aligned precisely so that each year at dawn on Samhain, sunlight streams in and hits the stone at the back of the passage.

Atop the Hill of Tara lies its largest monument, Ráith na Rí, a large oval enclosure built around 100 B.C. with two conjoined earthworks at its center.

It remains a great mystery not only how ancient people pulled off such an engineering feat, but why. Across Ireland, many tombs were aligned to important dates in the solar calendar, such as solstices, suggesting a spiritual purpose and connection to the dead. At Samhain in particular, the ancient Irish believed the Hill of Tara was a passage point between our world and the Otherworld. Could the sunlight illuminating the Mound of the Hostages tomb on Samhain have represented a special link between realms on that day? The answers are lost to time, but we do know that the Hill of Tara has remained important in celebrations of Samhain throughout Irish history, right up to today.

Another important site for the celebration of the Samhain festival—the progenitor of Halloween—lies less than 15 miles (25 km) away. The Hill of Ward is a large spiral earthwork monument, or ring fort, used as a ritual site since the Iron Age. Whereas Tara was seen as the seat of the high king, the Hill of Ward was the sacred place of Celtic religious leaders, known as Druids. In fact, the hill is also called Tlachtga, the name of a druidess who, in Irish mythology, gave birth to triplets on the hill.

Like the cave at Oweynagat (see page 53), Tlachtga was seen as a point of passage to the underworld, and the hill has a friendly competition with Rathcroghan as the "birthplace of Halloween." In reality, both sites were important at Samhain, with the cave seen as a place where spirits and magical creatures would emerge (thus, perhaps, a place to avoid that night) and the Hill of Ward as a place to gather. Each year the Druids would gather on Tlachtga, lighting a sacred bonfire for the gods. The flames of the old year were to be extinguished, and the great fire of Tlachtga would be carried on torches to light new fires throughout the countryside. The main conflagration was said to be visible from the Hill of Tara.

Modern-day spiritual pagans still gather on the Hill of Ward to celebrate Samhain, leaving candles and offerings on the stones atop the mounds. And in the neighboring towns of Trim and Athboy, the ancient roots of Halloween are now revived each year at the Púca Festival, an eerie celebration of the traditions of Samhain. It starts with fire performances and a parade of Irish mythological characters through the dark, narrow streets of the town of Trim. Festivalgoers embody the blend of Samhain and Halloween, with devil and witch costumes mixed in among ancient Irish characters like the Morrígan. It all culminates at a big-stage music festival—making this ancient place the hottest spot in the world to be on October 31, for the last few thousand years running.

⚕ BEFORE YOU GO

You can't enter the tomb in the Mound of the Hostages, but to experience the mystery of a 5,000-year-old passage tomb, visit nearby Newgrange, which is aligned to the winter solstice sun. This huge monument is about 1,000 years older than Egypt's pyramids, and on the December solstice, the rising sun casts a beam of light into its chamber for 17 minutes (if it's a sunny day in cloudy Ireland), a bit of magic that only a handful of people chosen by lottery get to see. But book a tour in advance and a guide will lead you into the dark inner chamber and turn on a light at the entrance that shows you the "solstice effect" any time of year.

St. Patrick's Purgatory

Legend says this remote island monastery was built atop an entrance to purgatory.

For more than 1,500 years, pilgrims have trekked to a small island in the middle of an Irish lake said to hold a pit leading to purgatory. For much of this time, it was a rite of passage for the faithful to spend a night locked in the purgatorial pit to face the torments of hell as an extreme form of penance. These days, the gateway to the underworld is covered over, but thousands of Catholics still flock each year to the pilgrimage site known as St. Patrick's Purgatory to renounce the devil, performing grueling rituals of penitence that date back to medieval times.

According to ancient legend, the patron saint of Ireland himself visited the island in the fifth century A.D. and called out to Christ for help converting the stubborn pagans to Christianity. Jesus, as the story goes, led Patrick to a cave that held an entrance to purgatory—the fiery in-between place where Catholic doctrine holds that souls go to be cleansed of any remaining sin before going on to heaven. Show them this, Jesus advised, and they'll see what they face in an afterlife without God.

The fifth-century missionary St. Patrick, though never formally canonized, is considered the patron saint of Ireland for working to convert the Irish to Catholicism.

It worked. Though today's scholars doubt Patrick ever truly visited Lough Derg, the lake where St. Patrick's Purgatory was built, the pit at the religious site proved a major draw to this remote outpost of Christianity.

These were the early days of Christianity's spread across Europe, and at that time Ireland was considered the literal end of the world. Perhaps that's why the mystics following St. Patrick went to Ireland. As they saw it, they were fighting back the devil by spreading the Gospel, as Jesus told his disciples to do in the first book of Acts, "to the ends of the earth."

The missionaries began to establish monasteries, including one in a seemingly unlikely place: a small island in the middle of a remote lake called Lough Derg in northwestern Ireland, where Druids were active. (It was common at the time for Christians to supplant the local pagan religions by setting up shop nearby). The original monastery was a small outpost built in the fifth century on Saints Island, next to the island with the purgatory pit.

Pilgrims began to come from all across Europe, spending two weeks on Saints Island to prepare themselves for the main event: being locked in the purgatory pit for 24 hours. This was a deadly serious ritual of penance, meant to purge the soul, says the current Prior of Lough Derg, La Flynn, standing on the grassy mound where the pit once was. Pilgrims went into the pit without food or drink for a full day, after two weeks of fasting. Before entering, a Requiem Mass was said for the pilgrims, and the Office of the Dead (a liturgy for the departed) was sung over them. "There was a sense that this might be it," he says. "You were prepared to meet your God."

Though pilgrims called it a "cave," Flynn says it was really not much more than a hole in the ground. Early pilgrims described descending about six stairs into a cavern about nine feet (3 m) long, then turning into a niche about half that size. The cramped conditions would force pilgrims to kneel—and likely contributed to the terror of being locked inside. The church constructed a small building over the pit that could be locked shut, and some of the pilgrims who wrote accounts of their time inside the purgatory described seeing and hearing demons and getting a glimpse of the horrors of hell itself. A Catalonian nobleman named Ramon de Perellós who made the pilgrimage in 1397 wrote one particularly vivid account:

A small island in Lough Derg is home to St. Patrick's Purgatory, a Catholic pilgrimage site where Jesus is said to have revealed an entrance to the underworld.

> Many things I saw in that purgatory, things which I was
> forbidden to tell on pain of death, and God forbid that they
> should be revealed by my mouth. He who would think on
> the afflictions and the torments which are there, would
> have them always in the memory of his heart; the travails
> and pains of this world or other sicknesses or poverty would
> not weigh them down for all the torments of this world are
> but sweet dews and sweet honey compared to those.

During his time in the pit, de Perellós described being led by
demons deep into the land of the dead, where he saw souls being nailed
to the ground, plagued by biting serpents and burning toads, and lying
on beds of burning nails.

Penitents spoke of all kinds of horrors in the pit, says Prior Flynn.
(Remember: They went in after two weeks without food.) Such a rite of
passage, or what some call "rites of terror," may have been a Christian-
ized version of pagan rituals, according to Irish archaeologist John
Waddell, following the model of ritual frightening of young Irish warriors by closing them up in the cave at Oweynagat (see page 53).

This long tradition has held up, in some fashion, today. Every summer, the faithful still return to Lough Derg. Their three-day pilgrimage
has been described as one of the most grueling in all of Christianity.
Pilgrims hold a 24-hour waking vigil and eat one simple meal a day of
toast and oat cakes. They spend much of their time rotating among nine
station prayers, walking barefoot and kneeling on rocky paths outdoors
while reciting prescribed prayers on repeat.

Though the island is bustling with thousands of Catholic pilgrims
in June, on a blustery, drizzly November day, the place feels lonely, the
basilica empty and echoing. Where the purgatorial pit once was, there's
now a small grassy hillock topped by a bell tower. That said, for a place

of penance, it's a truly lovely location. And those who choose to under-take the pilgrimage say it's a special and peaceful experience. No cell phones or other distractions are allowed, and pilgrims are advised to bring only a few basics, including warm clothing, insect repellent, and rosary beads.

BEFORE YOU GO

Plan ahead: Only pilgrims are allowed on the island during the pilgrimage season, from the beginning of June until mid-August. One-day and three-day pilgrimages are available for the faithful. The rest of the year, anyone can visit the lakeshore, where a small welcome center explains the history of the area and a walking tour along a path offers vantage points of the island. Several tour operators also offer seasonal boat trips and guided tours of the island.

Valley of Hinnom

This ancient hell is locked in a ravine in Jerusalem.

f you head west from Zion Gate at the southwestern edge of the Old City of Jerusalem, you'll reach a small green valley that runs south and then east around Mount Zion. It's called the Valley of Hinnom, and it's a peaceful stretch of green that deepens into rocky slopes. And yet the Valley of Hinnom has another name: Gehenna, which is translated as "hell" in the King James Bible. To ancient Israelites, the valley was the most abominable place imaginable: a deep ravine where parents sacrificed their children to pagan gods.

This dark history spawned many stories about the valley over the years, including that it burned with never-ending fires, into which all manner of refuse was disposed. The medieval rabbi David Kimhi wrote in the 13th century:

Gehenna is a repugnant place, into which filth and cadavers are thrown, and in which fires perpetually burn in order to consume the filth and bones; on which account, by analogy, the judgment of the wicked is called "Gehenna."

The Valley of Hinnom, just outside the walls of Jerusalem's Old City, has long been believed to be a place of evil where God punishes the wicked.

It's difficult to sort out how much of the filth and cadavers part is true, because there's no archaeological evidence that the valley was actually used as a trash dump.

According to some descriptions, there once was a bronze altar in the valley holding a statue shaped like the pagan god Moloch with his arms held aloft. The statue was open at the bottom to contain a fire. Once the fire got the statue scalding hot, a child would be laid in Moloch's outstretched arms while priests beat drums to drown out its cries. (Because of these rituals, Moloch is often depicted with a baby blazing in his belly.) The Judean king Josiah was so horrified by these sacrifices—and the worship of pagan gods by the Canaanites—that he banned all worship of gods other than the Jewish god, Yahweh. The pagan altars were destroyed, the valley considered forever desecrated.

By the time Jesus came onto the scene, the valley was infamous. Jesus warned that it would figure into the upcoming Last Judgment, in which God's enemies would be destroyed. In Matthew 10:28, he says that one should not "fear those who kill the body but cannot kill the soul; rather fear him who is able to destroy both soul and body in

Though biblical descriptions of hell are brief, writers and artists have richly imagined the details of eternal hellfire, as in this fresco at Bulgaria's Rila Monastery.

Gehenna." Gehenna became known as the place where God would one day annihilate the wicked. The Old Testament Book of Jeremiah called Gehenna the "valley of slaughter," the place where God would kill the wicked on Judgment Day and fill the valley with their corpses until there was room for no more.

That idea eventually morphed into Gehenna as a metaphor, or even a synonym, for Christian hell. In fact, most current translations of the New Testament don't use the word "Gehenna" at all, changing it to *hell*. This small shift has muddled the whole question of Jesus' actual take on hell, which some modern scholars argue probably hewed closer to the traditional Jewish notion of an apocalyptic judgment day for all rather than a place of punishment after death.

Today, you wouldn't guess the valley's dark history by looking at it. In 1974, Israel declared the area around the Old City, including the Valley of Hinnom, a national park. In Gehenna, you'll see children play and concertgoers stretch out on the valley's green grass. An education farm shows off ancient agricultural practices with a winepress and stone olive mill. It may not be hellish these days, but it's a great place to get a feel for the geography of ancient Jerusalem—and imagine the hell that was born here.

⚷ BEFORE YOU GO

For a scenic overview from Mount Zion, go to the Church of St. Peter in Gallicantu and look to the southwest to see the connecting Kidron and Hinnom Valleys. To explore the valley itself, Gey Ben Hinnom Park, south of Zion Gate, is a good place to start.

Houska Castle

A castle in the woods is said to protect the world from demons trying to escape hell.

t's quite a dilemma for a king: demons breaking out of hell through a deep crack in the earth. They're terrorizing the countryside, and the subjects are getting fed up. Worse, this gateway to hell is at the top of a steep cliff, surrounded by a dark, creepy forest in the middle of nowhere. What's a monarch to do?

If you're King Otakar II of Bohemia and you're fresh off a crusade against pagans, you might just build a big castle over the crack to seal it off. And—for good measure—put a Christian chapel on top of it.

It's still debated why the king built Houska Castle, sometime during his reign from 1253 to 1278. Most likely, the castle was constructed as an administrative building for managing royal estates—rather boring for a fortress against evil, but practical. Its remote location wasn't good for much else; it wasn't close to a border or trade routes, or even a reliable source of water.

But the structure may have also served a darker, more strategic purpose. In 1254, Otakar II, a Christian loyal to the Holy Roman Empire, led the first of two crusades against the Old Prussians, who worshipped pre-Christian (that is, pagan) deities. So he may have been quite aware of disturbing reports of demons and ungodly forces within his territory.

Legend holds that King Otakar II of Bohemia built Houska Castle
to block a fissure in the earth that acted as a passage to hell.

For centuries, folklore in the area had told of a deep crack in the limestone cliff where the castle sits. When locals tried to fill it with rocks,
they were terrified to discover anything they threw in would simply
disappear into a seemingly bottomless pit. Eventually, tales began to
circulate of strange half-human creatures emerging from the fissure

and winged beasts that flew overhead. This was surely a gateway to hell, people believed, and demons were escaping through it.

So, according to legend, the king had the castle built on this particular spot to block the hellish creatures forever. Not only did he cover the crack in the earth with a castle, but he built a chapel directly over the fissure and dedicated it to the archangel Michael, leader of God's army against Satan and his demons, offering physical *and* religious protection from whatever lurked beneath. It's said there remained an entrance to the pit of some kind, and that the king offered his prisoners a pardon if they agreed to be lowered into the pit and report back on what they saw. The first to do so supposedly entered as a young, healthy man but came back with white hair and wrinkles; there weren't many more volunteers after that.

Whatever its original purpose, the castle does have some unusual quirks: False windows are stoned up from the inside and the building's defensive walls face inward—with the thickest parts of the wall facing the interior—as though to keep something in, instead of out. The original castle was also never intended to be a residence; it was built with no kitchen and no stairs to the upper levels—for many years it sat unoccupied. Only after the castle was renovated into a chateau in the late 16th century did it become a home, housing members of nobility for many years before being bought in 1924 by the president of Škoda Auto, Josef Šimonek, whose descendants still own the property.

Today, the castle operates as a museum of sorts. Visitors can tour the castle and see a knight's drawing room and the demon-stopping chapel dedicated to the archangel Michael, including a fresco painting depicting a half-human creature from pagan mythology. There's plenty of creepy hell-themed decoration on-site, including a 39-foot-long (12 m) hand-carved wooden mechanical representation of hell based on scenes from Dante's *Inferno*. And if you dare, you can even stay overnight in the castle's game room, which is now outfitted to hold up to four guests.

Whether or not you believe there's anything supernatural about Houska Castle, it *has* had a dark history. Among its latter occupants was a notorious Swedish military commander named Oronto who was said to practice black magic. According to the rumors, Oronto performed rituals and animal sacrifices in the castle to tap into the evil powers below it. During World War II, Nazis occupied it, and more stories arose about occult activities that SS leader Heinrich Himmler and others practiced within its walls.

To this day, tales of ghosts and strange occurrences haunt the place. Some say that cars won't start in its vicinity and that voices and screams can be heard at night. None of this dissuades the tourists who come to see the famous "haunted castle," often in combination with the nearby Kokořín Castle, a picture-perfect medieval castle where you can take in stunning views from the turret. Visit both and take a walk in the deep, dark forests surrounding them; you'll feel like you've stepped straight into the pages of a dark and twisted fairy tale.

Hekla Volcano

A fiery eruption of this ice-topped volcano was seen as a sign from hell.

n a country known for its hot-tempered volcanoes, it says something that one was given the moniker "Gateway to Hell." Hekla earned its reputation with a series of explosive, unpredictable eruptions so fiery that medieval people across Europe took them as proof of hell's existence.

Located in southern Iceland, the volcano has erupted more than 20 times in the past thousand years, most recently in 2000. During an eruption, a long fissure opens along the length of the volcano, which is often said to look like an overturned boat, and spews enormous volumes of lava. Today, scientists say Hekla could erupt again at any time, but that doesn't stop tourists from coming to see the magnificent sight of the ice-capped volcano rising almost 5,000 feet (1,520 m) above sea level amid a landscape known for its hot springs, cobalt blue lakes, waterfalls, and lava fields.

Hekla came to be known as the Gateway to Hell after multiple eruptions during the Middle Ages, including a catastrophic blast around 1104 that spread ash and pumice across northern Europe. Christians of the time took note; they believed the eruption broke the barriers to hell. In 1120, a mysterious monk, known only by the name Benedeit, wrote a poem called "The Voyage of St. Brendan" describing a volcano of fire and ice that scholars suspect was Hekla. In the poem, the volcano is the personal hell of Judas Iscariot, who betrayed Jesus. (Imagining Judas's special torments in hell has long been a popular theme for writers, as in the ninth circle of hell in Dante's *Inferno;* see page 153.) Both in the mountain's fiery crater and on the

A 1585 map depicts a flaming Hekla, the volcano that came to be known as the Gateway to Hell after a series of violent eruptions in the Middle Ages.

icy mountainside, Judas is tortured on a daily cycle: On Wednesdays, for instance, he's dunked in boiling pitch, then staked between two fires on the mountain. On Thursdays, he's left in a frozen valley so cold that he longs to be back in the fires.

Throughout the next several centuries, eruptions came sporadically: sometimes a decade apart, sometimes closer to a century. But they were frequent enough that infernal legends continued to grow and spread. In the 16th century, German scholar Caspar Peucer wrote that the gates of hell could be found "in the bottomless abyss of Hekla Fell." He also described miserable cries and moans heard rising from Hekla, presumably those of suffering souls. In a 17th-century book by la Martinière, the devil is said to torture sinners by pulling them from Hekla's fiery crater and dipping them in the icy waters of the ocean. Even today, a legend holds that witches meet on the mountain during Easter.

In more recent years, Hekla has kept Iceland on its toes. An eruption in 1947 lasted more than a year, creating a river of lava. More recent eruptions have been highly explosive and unpredictable, sending plumes of ash and gases high into the atmosphere and disrupting air travel. The last major eruption included a dangerous pyroclastic flow with hot rock and ash rocketing from the eruption, destroying everything in its path.

For those willing to take the chance of another eruption, Hekla can be explored by helicopter, jeep, hiking to the top, or even skiing around the crater. But because it tends to erupt with little warning—sometimes less than 30 minutes from the first rumbles—most visitors opt for day trips of the Landmannalaugar area near the volcano, where you can take a dip in the hot springs and see the area's colorful rhyolite mountains streaked in pink, yellow, orange, and blue—and view Hekla from a distance. That way, you can make sure not to get too close a look at hell.

Well of Hell

A desert sinkhole is known as a gateway to Islamic hell.

This almost perfectly round black hole in the Yemeni desert looks as if someone tried to drill a hole straight to Earth's center. For those brave—or foolish—enough to peek over the edge, the view is usually a black abyss, as little light filters to the bottom unless the sun is right overhead. The eerie void, technically a sinkhole, is known as the Well of Barhout, but it also goes by a more ominous name: the Well of Hell.

According to folklore, the well imprisons a horde of spirits, known as jinn. In Islamic tradition, jinn are otherworldly beings created by Allah from a smokeless fire (by comparison, humans, in Islamic tradition, were created from earth). The jinn can be either good or evil—those in the well chose evil—and occupy Al-Ghaib, a realm of the unseen and unknowable, including both paradise (called Jannah) and hell (Jahannam). Jinn can appear in our realm as snakes or other animals, or even in human form.

In one origin story, the Well of Barhout was created by an infamous king named Shaddad bin Aad, who lived just after the time of Noah's Flood. According to legend, the king was vexed when he took over eastern Yemen and found only a dry desert. So he ordered two jinn to dig wells and channels to bring water to the surface, including what is now the Well of Barhout. Once the well was built, he began using it as a prison for unruly jinn. Eventually, the hole became known as a gateway to Jahannam, a place of inextinguishable flames fueled by the burning of the sinful.

According to local legends, water from the hole emits a foul smell, the screams of imprisoned jinn have been heard rising from it, and anything—or anyone—that gets too close can be sucked in. And that wouldn't end well: The gaping maw is almost 100 feet (30 m) across, and plunges 367 feet (112 m) deep.

A few bold cavers have ventured into the upper parts of the well over the years, but it wasn't until 2021 that explorers from the Oman Cave Exploration Team climbed all the way to the bottom. Geologist and caver Mohammed Al Kindi was the first person to descend. He reported an eerie, but fascinating, scene. Water percolates through the upper rock layers and then flows out of holes in the lower half of the sinkhole, creating waterfalls that pour down the walls. Minerals from the flowing water have gradually built up to form spiky stalagmites rising from the cave floor, as well as small jade green spheres known as cave pearls. The team also discovered a small, self-contained ecosystem at the bottom of the sinkhole, including beetles, toads, and nearly translucent snakes.

Video footage of the expedition shows the cavers dropping over an edge into the enormous hole on a slim rope and pulley, a heart-stopping sight. Once they reached the bottom, they could see the layered rock walls above lit by sunlight filtering in. The view from the bottom of the

An Omani team made the first known descent into the deep sinkhole known as the Well of Hell in 2021.

The Well of Barhout is an almost perfectly round hole nearly 100 feet (30 m) wide and 367 feet (112 m) deep in Yemen's desert, near the border of Oman.

Well of Hell was reportedly striking, eerily beautiful. Even though geologists say this is an ordinary—if rather deep—sinkhole, it's easy to see why one might take it as a portal to a terrifying underworld.

⛧ BEFORE YOU GO

Tourism has been limited in Yemen since 2011, when a political revolution kicked off what became a bloody civil war.

Mount Osore

This entrance to the underworld is one of Japan's most sacred spots.

The name of Mount Osore, known in Japan as Osorezan, translates as either Fear Mountain or Mount Dread. It's an appropriate name for an entrance to hell. Perched on an active volcano's scorched, bubbling, and smoking landscape, Osore is considered one of Japan's most sacred sites and a gateway to the afterlife, where souls cross a river to enter the underworld.

An ancient Buddhist temple sits atop Mount Osore. The temple was founded in the ninth century on the shores of Lake Usori, a highly sulfuric crater lake in the middle of the volcano's caldera. The lake's waters shimmer in beautiful shades of crystal blue, but they're acidic and toxic—so don't even think about jumping in. The gray, barren volcanic area surrounding it is shrouded in stinking sulfur mists and pockmarked by steaming hot springs and gurgling fumaroles, lending a spooky ambience.

Despite all this, and its status as a place of mourning, Osore is surprisingly popular with tourists. Like other active volcanic areas, the landscape is strange and foreboding but scenic. Some come to explore the mystical side of Japanese culture or to be moved by the human connection to the afterlife here, while others visit just to see such a strange and fascinating place.

The mountain bears a striking similarity to ancient descriptions of the Japanese Buddhist afterlife, which is portrayed as having eight mountain peaks and a river, the Sanzu-no-Kawa or Sanzu River, that must be crossed to enter the realm of the dead. Because of its location, the temple at Mount Osore is a *bodai-ji,* meaning it's dedicated to communion with the dead. In particular, the temple is important for families mourning children who have died. In Japanese Buddhism, the souls of children who die before their parents cannot cross the Sanzu River to the afterlife (similar to crossing the Styx of Greek mythology) because they have not had time to accumulate enough good deeds, or karma. Instead, they must be guided across the Riverbed of Death, or Sai no Kawara.

Twice a year, the temple holds religious festivals for mourners. Visitors line up to meet with *itako,* spiritual mediums who summon the souls of the dead and speak in their loved ones' voices. Traditionally, blind women trained for years to become itako as part of an ancient belief system that predates Japanese Buddhism (see page 88). The itako learn to communicate with Shinto spirits known as *kami,* including the spirits of the dead. Today, the tradition is fading, and only a handful of itako remain to provide their services at the festivals.

Other signs of the temple's significance for mourning pilgrims are found throughout the area. In the dry valley beyond the temple is a large collection of Jizo statues, cute round-faced figures that symbolize the guardian deity of children. Jizo protects these children in the afterlife from evil spirits. The statues are often adorned with red bibs and caps, as the color red is used to ward off evil in Buddhist tradition. Mourners also place brightly colored pinwheels as memorials to children who have died and stack piles of stones to help guide souls into the afterlife.

Mount Osore is a place of grief, but those who visit the sacred mountain are bound to be touched by the timeless traditions and surreal beauty.

At Mount Osore's temple, mourners place pinwheels as memorials to children who have died. Stacked stones and statues of Jizo, guardian deity of children, are meant to guide young souls to the afterlife.

⟨trident icon⟩ BEFORE YOU GO

The Bodai-ji Temple at Mount Osore is closed from November through April. The temple's festivals for the dead take place in late July and early October. Tourists are welcome to explore the lake, temple, and its grounds, and to soak in the temple's onsen baths, which are fed by hot springs (bring a towel). The temple also offers overnight lodging with two vegetarian meals. Visitors are allowed to attend the festivals or regular services in the main temple, where devotees pray for the souls of dead children. Services are in Japanese, and the same etiquette applies to Bodai-ji Temple as in other Japanese temples, including removing shoes before entering. The nearest town, Mutsu, offers restaurants, accommodations, and onsen baths open to tourism.

Japanese Hell

In ancient Japan, there was no hell. Shintoism, Japan's traditional belief system, holds that the world is made of spirits called *kami* that cause all natural phenomena, from winds and rain to life itself. A person who dies becomes a kami. The spirit realm in traditional Shinto includes a netherworld inhabited by vengeful spirits, such as those who died violently, but it's not a place of punishment.

By about the sixth century A.D., Buddhism gained traction in Japan, and its ideas of the afterlife began to take hold. Japanese Buddhists introduced the idea of a multilevel hell called Jigoku, which contains eight fiery hells and eight icy hells, each containing more sub-hells. Though Jigoku is not an eternal hell, but rather a stop on the revolving wheel of life and rebirth, it is firmly a place of judgment and punishment for one's misdeeds. It's ruled by Emma-ō, who wields a mystical mirror that reflects a soul's deeds and sins as well as a scale to weigh a soul's wickedness against its virtue.

Cape Reinga

Take a spiritual leap from the wild and beautiful tip of New Zealand.

Cape Reinga feels like a special and mystical place, no matter what you believe about the afterlife. From atop this windy promontory at New Zealand's far northwest point, you can watch major ocean currents collide, the bright blue and turquoise waters of the Tasman Sea and the Pacific Ocean rushing toward each other and mixing in white frothy peaks where they meet. In Maori mythology, this joining of the seas represents the union of male and female and the creation of life.

But this place also has another meaning for Indigenous Maori people. For them, this beautiful spot at the top of a cliff is known as Te Rerenga Wairua, meaning "the leaping place of the spirits." It is a gateway to the Maori version of the underworld, from which all *wairua* (spirits) are born and where they return after death.

The Maori underworld, Rarohenga, is nothing like the underworld or hell of many other cultures. It's not a dark and scary place, but rather a spiritual realm often described as full of peace and light. After death, Maori spirits fly to the leaping place at Cape Reinga and descend to the water by sliding along the roots of a pohutukawa tree. Then the spirits follow a path known as Te Ara Wairua, traveling beneath the ocean to

Three Kings Islands, just visible on the horizon from Cape Reinga. There, they climb out onto Ōhau, the islands' highest point, to take one last look back at their earthly home before passing on to the ancestral homeland.

Today, an ancient tree stands bent by the wind on a rocky outcrop at the bottom of Cape Reinga, visible down a steep hillside from the lighthouse on the cape's point. This sacred tree is called the kahika or Te Aroha. It's a pohutukawa tree with a crown of spreading, twisted

Maori people call New Zealand's northwest tip Te Rerenga Wairua, or "leaping place of the spirits," where souls of the dead plunge into the afterlife.

branches surviving in a seemingly impossible place, a small sandy spot nestled in a rock face lashed by salty winds. A survey in the 1960s put the tree at about 800 years old, which is about how long the Maori may have been in New Zealand.

According to Maori oral history, the great navigator Kupe was the first person from Hawaiki to discover New Zealand, and his wife originally named the land Aotearoa, or "land of the long white cloud," for the clouds that helped them find the islands. After landing near Cape Reinga, Kupe's crew settled the northern reaches of the island, and he established Te Rerenga Wairua as the leaping-off place from which his descendants' spirits would return to their ancestral homeland.

Maori people consider the site sacred, and many observe traditional burial practices, like sleeping in the community meetinghouse with the remains of a loved one, which lie in state for three days for final goodbyes. After that, the spirit is believed to go to Cape Reinga. On a tour of Cape Reinga, I asked my Maori bus driver if she believes spirits fly there. She paused and said she had been thinking about that more lately. Traditional beliefs about the afterlife might not be as strong among younger Maori, she said, but many do hold to the idea of Cape Reinga. And she believes her spirit will go to Cape Reinga to join her ancestors.

It's a beautiful idea of the underworld: an underwater journey to the great beyond that begins and ends with the welcoming arms of family.

🔱 BEFORE YOU GO

Visiting Cape Reinga is a small adventure in itself. From Auckland, the nearest major city, the cape is a nearly six-hour drive. But the drive on Route 1 from Auckland to Cape Reinga is a beautiful one, considered a classic route, offering the chance to see New Zealand's iconic kauri trees (decimated by logging and now protected) at the Puketi Forest, as well as the enormous sand dunes of Te Pake.

Cape Reinga has no town or settlement, no public transportation, spotty cell service, and only one public toilet. But from the tourist-friendly towns of the Bay of Islands a few hours away, touring flights as well as guided coach tours will drive along the packed sands of Ninety Mile Beach (actually closer to 50 miles/80 kilometers long, but who's counting?). Eating and drinking at the cape are discouraged given its sacred nature.

Maya Cenotes

You can dive right into the portals to the Maya underworld.

Scattered across the Yucatan Peninsula like thousands of blue jewels, cenotes are some of the most magical and otherworldly places on Earth. From above, a cenote may look like an ordinary cave entrance, or even just a hole in the ground, but inside, one enters a hidden world where shafts of light play against clear waters, dangling tree roots, and ribbonlike cave formations. These special places were important ritual sites for the ancient Maya people, who saw them as watery portals to the underworld, called Xibalba.

Cenotes are formed only under very special conditions in places with high rainfall and a calcium-rich limestone landscape. There are no rivers on the Yucatan Peninsula—at least, not aboveground. Instead, rainwater trickles through the porous stone into the earth and forms a thin layer of water—called a lens aquifer—that eventually carves intricate networks of caves filled with underground rivers and lakes. When the ceiling of a cave collapses, it creates a sinkhole, or cenote, open to the sky that fills with water. The peninsula has an estimated 6,000 or more cenotes, many open to visitors (some for a small fee) to swim, snorkel, or scuba dive.

The Maya have long considered caves of all kinds to be sacred as passages to the underworld, and cenotes are the most sacred of all,

combining the fundamental elements of earth and water in one powerful place. The Maya believed the rain god Chaac lived in caves and cenotes, scooping water from these vessels in the earth and pouring it from the sky as rain to give life to all living things. More practically, cenotes were also the only source of fresh water; some were designated for drinking water while others were used in religious rituals.

For the Maya, the sinkholes served as thresholds between this world and the nine-level underworld Xibalba, a subterranean realm overseen by 12 death gods. The cenotes became important places to communicate with the gods who lived in Xibalba. The famous Maya temple pyramid Chichén Itzá, for instance, was built on a sacred cenote believed to lead to the underworld. Archaeologists have found gold, jewels, and the remains of more than 200 bodies buried at the bottom of the cenote, suggesting that devotees offered precious items, included human sacrifices, to Chaac by throwing them in.

Much of what we know about Xibalba comes from the Popol Vuh, a sacred text that describes the history and mythology of the K'iche' people, one of several Maya groups in Central America. The book describes Xibalba, whose name translates to the "place of fear," as a watery underworld where the dead face a series of physical challenges, plus a set of judgy, torturing deities.

The only way to avoid Xibalba (or Mictlán, for the Aztec) was to die a violent but noble death, such as in battle, during childbirth, or as a human sacrifice—a kind of cosmic consolation prize. Everyone else, however virtuous they were during life, was expected to suffer the trials of Xibalba, which is why the Maya buried their dead with survival kits for the afterlife that included food, tools, and weapons. The trials began

The Yucatan Peninsula's unusual geology has created thousands of cenotes, water-filled sinkholes so otherworldly that the Maya see them as portals to their underworld, Xibalba.

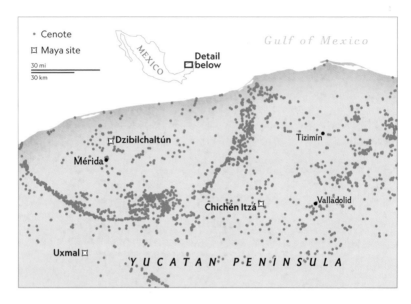

• Cenote
⊡ Maya site

30 mi
30 km

Gulf of Mexico

MEXICO

Detail
⊡ below

⊡ Dzibilchaltún

Tizimín•

Mérida•

Chichén Itzá ⊡

•Valladolid

Uxmal ⊡

Y U C A T A N   P E N I N S U L A

Data suggests there are upwards of 6,000 cenotes throughout Mexico's Yucatan Peninsula, which is also home to sacred Maya sites including Chichén Itzá and Uxmal.

with the harrowing journey into Xibalba, a passage through a treacherous labyrinth crisscrossed by rivers of scorpions, blood, and pus.

Once you reached Xibalba, things didn't look up. The 12 death gods who ruled the underworld worked in pairs to cause suffering for the dead. These Lords of the Underworld included ghoulish specialists in pain and disease such as Pus Master, Scab Master, Blood Gatherer, and Jaundice Master. The dead had to contend with them in each level via harrowing tests with fire, jaguars, and a game played with balls covered in sharp blades. Only those who successfully navigated the entire course could make their way back to the land of the living through the cycle of rebirth; the rest were stuck in Xibalba.

Christianity began to influence Maya ideas of the afterlife after Spanish contact in the early 1500s. Xibalba became more of a place of judgment and punishment; the worse one had been while alive, the

Hells of the Americas

As ancient people spread across North and South America and established their own cultures, they developed their own ideas about the afterlife. For Native Americans in North America, death could hold any number of outcomes, depending on a tribe's beliefs: One might be reincarnated, become one of the stars, or pass into a spirit world with dream links to the living, to name a few options.

Meanwhile, ancient Mesoamerican people had their own versions of the afterlife and underworld. The Maya civilization (which at the time was considered not one culture, but many groups) developed a unique view of the universe, with a flat world resting on the back of a crocodile. Above the earth lay 13 heavens, and below it, nine layers of the underworld, of which Xibalba, underworld of the dead, was one.

The Aztec likewise had a nine-level underworld, theirs called Mictlán. But their version of the afterlife adds a psychopomp (guide of souls) named Xolotl who leads the dead to the underworld, like Charon of Greek mythology. For them, this was where the dead navigated a hellish obstacle course that included mountains crashing into one another and a river of blood.

The Inca, meanwhile, divided the universe into just three realms: this earth (kay pacha), the world above (hanan pacha), and the world below (uku pacha). They, too, had a death god who ruled the underworld, named Supay. After the Spanish invasion and conquest of the Inca Empire, missionaries recast those realms in terms of the Christian ideas of heaven and hell, and Supay became associated with Satan or the devil.

longer one would stay there. In modern-day Maya communities, different ethnic groups have a variety of beliefs about the afterlife and practices for helping the dead navigate whatever comes next for them.

BEFORE YOU GO

Many cenote operators charge a small admission to take a dip in their cool waters. Several are open to visitors on tours of Chichén Itzá, but note that the Sacred Cenote (Cenote Sagrado) does not allow swimming. You can also get away from crowds by seeking out one of the many jungle cenotes through the various outfitters offering tours. Keep in mind that these are delicate ecosystems and an important source of fresh water for the region—never touch the stalactites and stalagmites in caves, and avoid wearing sunscreen or anything else that could contaminate the water.

Actun Tunichil Muknal

Journey into a cave where human sacrifices were
made to underworld gods.

D eep in the jungle of Belize, a dark keyhole-shaped cavern opens
into a passage to the ancient Maya underworld, where crystal-
line skeletons glisten in the light of explorers' headlamps as
reminders of human sacrifices made more than 1,000 years ago. It's
about as close to an *Indiana Jones* movie as it gets in real life.

To get to the cave, you first hike 45 minutes through the jungle of
Tapir Mountain Nature Reserve with three river crossings, one of which
often requires pulling yourself along a rope through cold, chest-high
water. By the time you reach the cave's entrance, you're soaked, which
is fine because inside you still have to wade another kilometer of a river
that winds through the cave before you step onto dry land again. Next
you squeeze past boulders and through the cave's largest chambers,
some more than 70 feet (20 m) in height. The passable part of the cave
system is about three miles long (5 km). Finally, you near the back of
the cave, where the crystallized human remains are found.

This is Actun Tunichil Muknal, ATM for short, a cave near the town
of San Ignacio that locals also refer to simply as Xibalba, the Maya version of hell. Extensive archaeological research has linked the cave to
Maya legends of Xibalba that describe rivers of blood, scorpions, and

pus amid a vast subterranean labyrinth ruled over by the Maya death gods (see page 93).

From about A.D. 250 to 900, the peak of Maya civilization, people would bring offerings to the cave for the gods who lived in Xibalba, the most important of whom was Chaac, god of life-giving rains. Early on, these offerings mostly consisted of food and pottery placed near the cave's entrance. In later years, when an intense drought parched the land, Maya priests began going deeper into the cave and sacrificing their own blood. They pierced their tongues or foreskins and let the blood drip onto bark paper, which was burned to release its spiritual essence into the cave.

Even still, the drought was unrelenting. Desperate, the people began to offer the gods the ultimate sacrifice: themselves. The Maya believed it an honor to be sacrificed to Chaac, as the victim would bypass Xibalba and be transported straight to the Maya version of heaven. As a result, children and people of noble status were often granted the honor.

The deepest part of ATM cave preserves the remains of 14 human sacrifices, including men and women, and children as young as toddlers. It's not clear how all of them were killed, but some died from savage blows to the head. Jaime Awe, a Belizean and the first archaeologist to explore the cave, described being "dumbfounded" when his light first shined on the skeleton of what appeared to be a young woman, perfectly intact and covered in calcium-based crystals that gave a subtle sparkle to the bones.

That calcified skeleton came to be known as the Crystal Maiden (though "she" eventually was confirmed to be a teenage "he"—now

Evidence of sacrifices to underworld gods was discovered in Actun Tunichil Muknal, including apparent human sacrifices such as this skeleton, known as the Crystal Maiden.

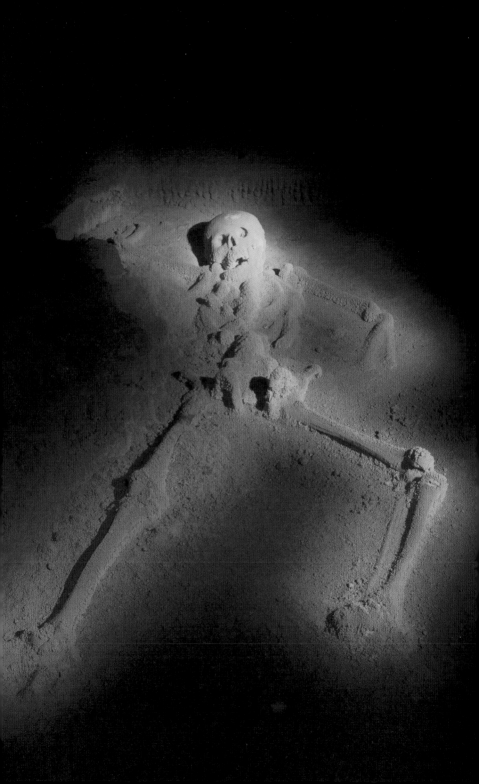

sometimes called the Crystal Prince). And the calcite crystals covering those bones and other artifacts in the cave (including sharp rock blades and bowls possibly used in draining the victim's blood) inspired its name: Actun Tunichil Muknal translates to "cave of the crystal sepulchre"—a sepulchre being a burial chamber. The crystals, which form when calcium minerals in the cave's water are deposited onto surfaces over time, have helped to preserve the Crystal Maiden and the 13 others. Together with cave carvings and other historical artifacts, the remains in ATM tell the tale of the last harrowing years of the great Maya civilization.

⚕ BEFORE YOU GO

You can book a day trip to ATM cave from most cities in Belize. Plan ahead: You can only enter the cave with a licensed guide, and the number of visitors per day is limited.

Masaya Volcano

See the boiling lava lake that inspired
medieval visions of hell's lake of fire.

When Spanish conquistadors first saw the lava lake in Masaya's crater, they wrote home to tell their king they had discovered La Boca del Infierno, the "Mouth of Hell." And the Spaniards didn't mean this figuratively; they saw diabolical activity at work. This was the 16th century, and very few Europeans had ever even seen a volcano, much less one holding a glowing lake of fire. To that group of God-fearing Christians, it must have indeed looked like the gateway to a Biblical inferno.

In 1525, a governor named Pedro Arias Dávila wrote to Emperor Charles V describing Masaya, located near the western coast of what is now Nicaragua. It was the first sighting by a European of a volcano in the Americas, and it made quite an impression: "... there is a large mouth of fire which never ceases to burn and during the night it is so big as if it reaches the sky, and with a height of 15 leagues [75 km] there is light as if it was day ... "

Masaya was, and still is, an unusual volcano because of its lava lake. Normally, erupting lava quickly cools when it hits the air and hardens into a solid plug, sealing off a volcano's vent until pressure builds high enough inside to blast through again. That pressure build often takes years or centuries. To form a lava lake and keep it molten, the heat of the volcano has to be perfectly in balance with the rate of cooling at the surface. Because these conditions are so unusual, there are currently only eight known persistent lava lakes in the world (see page 140).

Today, it's possible to walk through empty lava tubes created by past eruptions, emerge at the top of Masaya, and look down upon a lava lake that appeared in 2015 in the Santiago crater, one of four main craters on the volcano. It's an extraordinary sight, with lava churning and spitting high above your head—and far above that, you might even spot green parrots nesting in the crater walls.

Visitors may marvel at the geology of the site, but the Spanish weren't the first to see something both menacing and divine in the mountain's orange glow. Before they arrived, several Indigenous groups, including the Nicarao people, occupied the lands around Masaya for centuries. They saw the volcano as a god itself, and the home of a powerful sorceress. Her name was Chalchiuhtlicue, and she was a water deity borrowed from Mexican mythology. According to the Spaniards, the Nicarao people made sacrifices to the gods of the volcano, throwing young women and children into the fiery crater.

This led the Spaniards to double down on their conviction that not only were the Indigenous gods a product of the devil, but the volcano itself must also be a gateway to his lair. Friar Toribio de Benavente wrote that Masaya "must be the mouth of Hell and its fire must be supernatural and hellish, and the place from which the condemned are thrown by the demons."

Since the Spanish invasion, the lava lake on Masaya has come and gone several times—so it's not exactly permanent, but certainly persistent. Catch this sight when you can; no one knows when the lava lake might make its next disappearing act.

Masaya's fiery lava lake has been bubbling for centuries, inspiring terrified Spanish conquerors to name it La Boca del Infierno, or the "Mouth of Hell."

🔱 BEFORE YOU GO

Masaya Volcano National Park is Nicaragua's largest national park and home to two volcanoes, Masaya and Nindiri. To see the lava lake on Masaya, the easiest route is to climb the 280 concrete steps to the lookout point Mirador Cruz de Bobadilla. The spot holds a cross in the same spot where Friar Francisco de Bobadilla, of the Order of Our Lady of Mercy, planted one in 1528 to exorcise the demon from the mouth of hell.

Seven Gates of Guinee

New Orleans' cemeteries hold a series of
passages into voodoo's land of the dead.

Seven nights, seven moons,
seven gates, seven tombs.
—Voodoo cemetery chant

New Orleans is a city of mysteries and magic, a city where voodoo queens, saints, and spirits dance in the streets together. The blend of African, European, and Native American cultures that built the Big Easy also forged unique traditions, from the Mardi Gras Indians and jazz funerals to a distinct religion known as New Orleans voodoo. And according to some, the heart of the city holds the Gates of Guinee, a set of seven passages through which one can enter voodoo's realm of the dead.

Some practitioners of voodoo see the gates as metaphorical, but those who believe they have a physical location say they're in various cemeteries around New Orleans. The souls of the dead must visit all seven gates in a particular order, the story goes, to find their way to a guide,

New Orleans is known for aboveground tombs, like these at St. Louis Cemetery No. 1. The tombs prevent grave flooding—and add to the city's eerie ambience.

who will then lead them to the underworld known as Guinee or Guinea. The dead must pass through Guinee before reuniting with the ancestor spirits who look after their families in the world of the living.

There is, though, a catch. Spirit guards stand watch at the gates to keep the living from entering before their time has come. And if one were to go in the wrong order, or at the wrong time, malevolent spirits could cross into the land of the living, snatching up the unlucky and dragging them back to the underworld. So for any soul attempting to enter Guinee, it's important to follow the advice of the traditional cemetery chant: "Seven nights, seven moons, seven gates, seven tombs." This is taken to mean that along with being visited in the right order, the gates—believed to be located at certain tombs around the city's French Quarter—must be visited over the course of seven days. At each gate, the gatekeeper must be appeased with appropriate offerings and supplication. A spirit known as Baron Samedi, who aids in the final crossing, guards the last gate. (Baron Samedi, it's said, is particularly fond of rum and tobacco and is often depicted smoking a cigar.)

The African religion of Vodou arrived in New Orleans in the early 1700s with enslaved African people who brought their gods and beliefs with them. Vodou is a nature-based religion, with a female creator and the vodun, spirits who govern the forces of nature and can help or hinder humans. In their worship, Vodou believers perform rituals using objects inhabited by the divine spirits, such as animal parts; their enslavers saw these "fetishes" as strange and sinister.

So it came to pass that in 1724, the Louisiana Territory enacted its first Black Codes, or Code Noir, which governed the practices of enslavement and mandated Catholicism as the sole religion. All enslaved people were forcibly baptized and their native religions were strictly banned. And so, Vodou went underground—but it didn't disappear.

Voodoo, Vodou, Hoodoo, Vodun

The word "voodoo" is often used to invoke something mysterious or sinister, as in "voodoo economics." But the voodoo offered up as entertainment to tourists is actually a sensationalized version of one of the world's oldest religious traditions, known as Vodou or Vodun, an African religion that spread to the Americas with enslavement and blended with Catholicism to become the distinct practice now known as voodoo or vodou.

The roots of voodoo lie in the former West African kingdom of Dahomey, now Benin, and may go back 6,000 years, anthropologists say. The traditional religion of Vodou was brought to the Caribbean and the Americas with enslaved people, where it morphed across the diaspora as it mixed with local cultures. Today, voodoo refers to a group of African diasporic traditions with an estimated 50 or 60 million followers and a range of practices that are quite distinct in different places, such as in Haiti versus the southern United States. Accordingly, some practitioners use spelling to distinguish between Haitian Vodou versus New Orleans voodoo or vodun.

Further confusing things is hoodoo, which is the practice of a southern folk magic that's deeply tied to African American history. Like voodoo, it's drawn from African practices, but hoodoo is not religious. Hoodoo practitioners are also called root workers or conjure doctors, and use herbs, candles, animal parts, and body fluids to perform rituals and create charms. Some voodoo practitioners also use hoodoo, but hoodoo is used far more broadly by people of various religions.

Marie Laveau, thought to be pictured here,
was the most famous voodoo practitioner in New Orleans.

The newly converted enslaved peoples discovered similarities between their own religions and Catholicism, and began to veil their worship behind the Catholic veneration of saints. For instance, the *loa* (also written as *lwa)* or spirit known as Papa Legba, who in Africa guarded crossroads and entrances, was syncretized to St. Peter, who in Catholicism holds the keys to heaven's gate. Likewise, St. Expeditus— the patron saint of those in dire need—is often associated with Baron Samedi, who's often depicted as a skeleton with a top hat and tails and who presides over Guinee, waiting for souls at the seventh gate. To this day, candles depicting Catholic saints and symbolism are used in voodoo ceremonies.

As for finding the gates, some say that the ritual symbol (known as a *veve* or sigil) that represents Baron Samedi provides a map. By lining up the symbol's cross with the main streets of the French Quarter, the seven stars in the veve are thought to reveal the locations of the seven gates. And all are within the city's oldest cemeteries.

But even if you don't fancy a trip to Guinee, or to meet its guardians, New Orleans' "Cities of the Dead" are well worth seeing. Hundreds of ornate aboveground tombs date back centuries. The city's oldest remaining cemetery, St. Louis Cemetery No. 1, dates to 1789 and is where 19th-century voodoo practitioner Marie Laveau is believed to be buried in the tomb of her husband's family, the Glapions. Laveau was famous in her day as a healer and spiritual leader, and has been memorialized in song, film, and art as the original "voodoo queen."

Seven Gates of Hell

The idea of a trapdoor to hell in rural Pennsylvania seems just too good for people to pass up.

The otherwise non-spooky township of Hellam in southern Pennsylvania has been persistently rumored to be a portal to hell. Like the seven Gates of Guinee in New Orleans, this legend also has seven gates that lead to an underworld. And if you step through all seven gates in the woods northwest of town, you instantly land in hell.

No one is exactly sure how the story started, but it might have something to do with the name Hellam, which was originally Hallam, named for an area in England. Perhaps thinking the town had been named for hell, someone started the rumor that an insane asylum once in the area had caught fire, trapping the inmates within its seven locked gates. Another version holds that beyond a particular gate (the entrance to a private property), a series of further gates led to the entrance of hell.

In reality, the township never had an asylum, and the gate to the private property was just a normal gate. But because of all the trespassers looking for an entrance to the underworld, the gate in question has been removed, so now there's nothing to see. The citizens of Hellam Township

Legend holds that a passage through seven secret gates
in the Pennsylvania woods leads straight to hell.

have expressed frustration with their quiet town's spooky reputation, and
their website attempts to dissuade visitors who continue to hunt for the
gates: "This area is private property. Trespassers will be prosecuted."

PART TWO

HELLS

— ON —

EARTH

Now that we've learned a lot about hells—and entry points to them—you might be wondering: What about the really *hellish* places? You know, those destinations that will impress your friends and concern your mom. The hottest, scariest, most extreme places on the planet. The ones with fire and brimstone. Or at least the ones where you can get a T-shirt that says "I went to hell and all I got was this lousy T-shirt." Well, here they are.

Even though some of these places were never considered portals to the underworld or tied to any particular ancient lore, they have landscapes and features that remind us of hell: scorching heat, noxious gases, forbidding waters, or any number of menacing landforms. These are hells on Earth. After all, most of our ideas about what hell is came from real-world places.

In Dante's *Inferno,* the nine circles of hell are almost like a tour of the most awesomely awful places on Earth. There's a pit of fire, stinking pools, a scorched wasteland, and even an icy lake where the worst of the worst are trapped (see Dante's *Inferno,* page 153). All these places

During an explosive eruption like this one at Venezuela's Calbuco in 2015, collisions of rock, ash, and lava can produce lightning.

PAGE 114: More than a third of Yellowstone National Park sits above an active volcano, as evidenced by the steaming landscape of Midway Geyser Basin.

have real-world analogues, and adventurous travelers can experience them up close.

Some are fiery hells, like the world's eight modern-day lava lakes (page 140). The Gates of Hell in Turkmenistan (page 120) is a huge pit that has been burning in the middle of a desert for decades. To stand at the edge of any of these places is to come as close as one can to hell in a lifetime.

Others are flamboyant, without being in flames. In New Zealand, there are volcanic fields full of color and steam and geysers (page 176). There was once even a sparkling candy-colored geological wonder of the world, the Pink and White Terraces, now lost forever in an eruption that created a wholly new, and surreal, valley landscape with its own hellish features.

Some places embrace the idea of hell, even if they aren't particularly hellish. Hell, Michigan (page 130) is a perfectly nice little community outside the college town of Ann Arbor, but it has taken its name and run with it. You can get married in Hell, send a postcard from Hell, or even own a small piece of Hell. Halfway around the world, Singapore's Haw Par Villa (page 173) has a more serious bent, presenting moral lessons about Buddhist hell in a theme-park format; families and schoolchildren wander through a re-creation of the various tortures meted out to sinners in the afterlife.

Other places just can't seem to escape their ties to the underworld. Take for instance Naples, Italy, a scrappy, bustling city that's home to both the world's best pizza and a long history with hell (page 147). I visited Naples, planning to see one of the most famous portals to the underworld in ancient lore (the Cave of the Sibyl, page 41), but was surprised to find references to hell, purgatory, and the afterlife all over the city. One of the most unique spots was a church built for the express purpose of helping souls of the dead escape from purgatory. Naples was also important to Dante Alighieri, who likely took inspiration for his 14th-century epic *Inferno* from the city's surroundings in one of the world's most active volcanic zones, the Phlegraean Fields.

I love that Neapolitans describe themselves as superstitious ... and a bit morbid. Every corner seemed to hold some version of the evil eye (great for warding off demons or evil, in general) and the *corno* (or *cornicello*), a horn-shaped talisman often fashioned in red, a Middle Age symbol of both good luck and protection from the devil. I felt like I was among people who understood my weird fascinations.

Which is to say, I don't mean any slight to the places I'm calling hells on Earth. These are some of the most wondrous places travelers can visit. On the North Island of New Zealand, for instance, I found some of the most beautiful and vibrant landscapes I've ever seen—but they are equally hellish! I'll never forget the quiet little park downtown in Rotorua where visitors can dunk their feet in a relaxing hot spring, while sinister-looking fumaroles hiss steam into the air all around. Turns out, hell can be both relaxing *and* beautiful.

The world is full of these lovely little pieces of hell, just waiting for adventurous spirits willing to venture off more well-trod trails. So let's enjoy some of the most infernal, strange, and inspiring points on the globe.

Gates of Hell

Camp next to a blazing inferno in the middle of the desert.

Topping any bucket list of hellish destinations is a flaming pit carved into the middle of a Turkmenistan desert. Known simply to most as the Gates of Hell or Door to Hell, this 230-foot-wide (70 m) hole in the ground has been belching fire for more than 50 years. It really does look as if hell's ceiling has started to cave in.

The 66-foot-deep (20 m) pit is more officially known as the Darvaza gas crater, Darvaza being the nearest village in this fairly remote region of the Karakum Desert. (The Turkmen capital, Ashgabat, lies about 160 miles [260 km] south.) The desert covers roughly 70 percent of Turkmenistan and consists mostly of barren sand dunes that stretch as far as the eye can see. That desolate setting makes coming across a giant pit of flames that can be seen for miles all the more shocking.

The exact origins of the hellhole are mysterious. As the most commonly told story goes, Soviet geologists were drilling for oil in the desert in 1971, when they hit a pocket of natural gas. The drilling caused the ground to collapse into the pocket, creating the crater. Assuming the gas would burn itself out, the drillers decided to light it on fire. It never went out and the inferno has burned ever since.

No one is certain when or how this pit in the middle of a desert was set ablaze, but a natural gas seep below has kept it burning for several decades.

Some local geologists dispute this version of events, however, claiming the crater formed in the 1960s and was set on fire in the 1980s to burn off toxic gases fouling the area.

Either way, the crater has been burning for decades and shows no sign of fizzling out—unless the Turkmenistan government has something to do with it. In 2022, President Gurbanguly Berdymukhammedov asked geologists to figure out how to extinguish the Gates of Hell—despite its draw as a popular attraction in a country that gets little tourism otherwise. But the president cited health and environmental effects of the burning sinkhole as reasons to put it out.

It's not clear whether extinguishing the flames is possible, much less technically feasible. The underground gas reserve feeding the

Hell's Gates

The visual of a gate to hell is so powerful that many places have adopted it as a name. Here are a few of the best known Hell's Gates around the world:

HELL'S GATE GEOTHERMAL PARK IN ROTORUA, NEW ZEALAND: This volcanic area has steaming cliffs, sulfur pools, and mud baths you can relax in (see page 176).

HELLS GATE STATE PARK IN LEWISTON, IDAHO: Explore a passageway into Hells Canyon, North America's deepest canyon (at 7,900 feet/2,400 m), which the Snake River flows through and the Seven Devils Mountains border.

HELL'S GATE IN DEATH VALLEY, CALIFORNIA: An overlook marks the entry into scorching-hot Death Valley (see page 125).

HELL'S GATE NATIONAL PARK IN KENYA: The park is known for its geothermal activity as well as its namesake Hell's Gate Gorge, where a gap in red cliffs makes an apt "gate."

flames is so large that efforts to cap it have thus far proven futile. And even if the flames could be permanently put out, the site would continue to leak large amounts of methane, a powerful greenhouse gas, into the atmosphere. As it stands, the fires burn off that methane, converting it to carbon dioxide, which is less potent in its global warming effects. Scientists have even found bacteria that have adapted to living in the extreme environment with high temperatures and methane levels.

In the meantime, the Gates of Hell continues to be a draw for the relatively few tourists who visit Turkmenistan. It's a popular stop on tours that also explore the rich history of the region, which once lay at the heart of the Silk Road linking the Mediterranean to the Far East. After visiting the marble city of Ashgabat (home to the world's highest density of white marble-clad buildings in the world), you can travel by off-road vehicle into the desert to witness the fiery spectacle firsthand.

One explorer even took the ultimate step into hell. As part of a 2013 expedition partly funded by the National Geographic Society, George Kourounis donned a silvery flame-resistant suit, attached himself to a harness, and lowered himself into the fire. Imagine a foil-wrapped baked potato hovering over the flames of a gas grill, and that's about what it was like.

Kourounis, speaking with me in 2017 about the experience, said that even after years of exploring active volcanoes and chasing tornadoes, the Darvaza crater was intimidating. "The very first time I walked

Explorer George Kourounis was the first person ever to enter the Door to Hell. Wearing a heat-resistant suit, he collected soil to look for signs of life.

up to the edge and felt the heat, my first reaction was, I don't know if I'm going to be able to do this." He did go through with it, though, and said it was terrifying but beautiful. Surrounded by hundreds of hot-burning fires, Kourounis descended to the bottom of the crater and collected soil samples.

No one has yet repeated that experience. But for the lucky few who get to spend a night camped next to the Gates of Hell, it's a once-in-a-lifetime opportunity that comes with wicked bragging rights.

⟱ BEFORE YOU GO

Until someone figures out how to extinguish the Gates of Hell, visiting is still possible. You'll need a tourist visa to Turkmenistan (journalists, it's said, are not particularly welcome) and an approved guide. Outfitters are available to take guests through the desert via a four-wheel-drive to camp by the crater, or on a day trip from Ashgabat.

Hell's Gate

One of Earth's hottest places lives up to its name.

There's a little game you play as you approach Hell's Gate, an observation point near the eastern side of Death Valley National Park. It goes like this: Roll down your window, stick your arm out, and feel the temperature rise. And rise. And rise.

As you make the gentle descent from the desert peaks at the Nevada-California border, the heat will start to slowly increase. When you drop into Death Valley itself at Hell's Gate, the temperature suddenly shoots up by 10 to 20°F (5.6 to 11°C). Sink into it. You're entering the hottest, driest, and lowest spot in North America.

Lore often tells us hell is a hotbed, and Hell's Gate lives up to that promise. Located in the northern Mojave Desert, Death Valley is one of the hottest places on the planet (or *the* hottest, depending how you measure it). The valley reaches blistering summer temperatures because of its unusual geology. It sits below sea level, and the Sierra Nevada mountains to its west block any moist air coming from the Pacific Ocean. Mountains to the east further seal off the narrow valley, trapping hot air inside.

Thanks to these geological quirks, summer temperatures in Death Valley regularly exceed 113°F (45°C). On July 10, 1913, a blistering air temp of 134.1°F (56.7°C) recorded at the valley's Furnace Creek area set a world record, though that measurement's accuracy has been disputed. Not counting the 1913 record, the next highest would be a reliably measured temperature of 130°F (54.4°C), set on July 9, 2021.

Mountains surrounding Death Valley trap hot air and
make this one of the hottest places on the planet.

Hell's Gate is the point where the eastern mountains open into the valley, creating a virtual "gateway" to Death Valley. There's no actual gate, just a small area marked "Hell's Gate," where you can pull off the road and visit a park information center across the highway, yet it's

California's Sunny Hell

Death Valley's furnace-blasted landscape has inspired a number of hell-themed place-names. When you visit the area, make sure to check these out:

THE DEVIL'S CORNFIELD: California's Highway 190 winds through Death Valley National Park, and just east of Stovepipe Wells lies this plain dotted with clumps of arrowweed that resemble bundles of cornstalks after a harvest. The plant's roots hold on to the precious desert soil to survive, building up the mounds on which the plants sit.

DEVIL'S GOLF COURSE: Don't bring your golf clubs. This salt pan on the valley floor was reputedly first named in a 1934 National Park Service guidebook that said "only the devil could play golf" amid the many large halite salt crystal formations studding the otherwise flat landscape.

DANTE'S VIEW: Named for a view the medieval author of *Inferno* would have appreciated, this spot overlooks both Badwater Basin, the lowest dry point in North America, and Telescope Peak, which rises 11,331 feet (3,454 m) above sea level. From one to the other, it is the largest topographic relief in the contiguous United States.

DEVIL'S GATE GORGE AND DAM, LA CAÑADA FLINTRIDGE: If your travels take you to the Los Angeles area, check out a rock face with an eerie resemblance to the devil in profile. The spot has been the subject of many tales over the years, thanks not only to the rock, but also to the flowing waters said to make a creepy laughing sound.

The Hottest Places on Earth

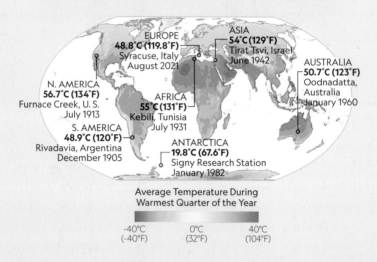

Average Temperature During Warmest Quarter of the Year

-40°C (-40°F)   0°C (32°F)   40°C (104°F)

The World Meteorological Organization has long bestowed the title of "hottest place on Earth" to aptly named Furnace Creek in Death Valley, California, which hit 134°F (56.7°C) on July 10, 1913. As recently as August 2020 and July 2021, Furnace Creek again hit 130°F (54.4°C), the highest air temperature recorded since a spot in Tunisia surpassed that mark in 1931.

But if you measure surface temperature instead of air temperature, two places bump Death Valley out of first place: the Lut Desert in Iran and the Sonoran Desert at the U.S.-Mexico border. Surface temperature, measured by satellites, is the temperature of the soil or ground cover. Just as the sand on a beach can be much hotter than the air above it, surface temps can reach blistering heights. Both places have hit surface highs of 177.4°F (80.8°C).

Meanwhile, the Dallol region in northern Ethiopia has long been considered the hottest *inhabited* place on Earth (see page 197), with an average year-round temperature of 95°F (35°C). Some of the other hottest places include the Sahara, Sonoran, Lut, and Gobi.

well worth a stop. The Hell's Gate overlook offers sweeping views across the valley's Mesquite Flat sand dunes and the cracked clay of an ancient lake bed, all the way to the Panamint Range on the valley's western side.

⚱ BEFORE YOU GO

The most comfortable time to visit Death Valley is from November through March, when temperatures typically stay in the 50 to 80°F (10 to 27°C) range. Summer temperatures can be dangerously hot, and there have been heat-related deaths in the park. For this reason, hiking should be done at higher elevations or before 10 a.m. The viewpoint at Hell's Gate is located at the intersection of Daylight Pass Road and Beatty Road, across from an information area for Death Valley National Park.

Hell

This small town has a helluva good time with its name.

According to Wikipedia, Hell has no boundaries, and its population is unknown. But according to lifelong denizen John Colone, Hell originally sat on 1,000 acres (405 ha) and today has claimed at least 72 souls—the unincorporated community's unofficial count of residents that Colone describes as a collection of "hellions, hellbillies, and wannabes."

Hell, Michigan, is an unincorporated settlement in the southeastern part of the state, west of Ann Arbor and Detroit. It's in a lovely area—Hell Creek (aka Portage Creek) runs through the town and connects to a chain of five lakes. The town grew up around a gristmill and distillery, and got a reputation for supplying locals with booze, which may have contributed to its name.

On that front, no one is certain how Hell came to be called Hell, but the most widely embraced legend is that after Michigan became a state in 1837, local landowner George Reeves was asked to put an official name to his plot of land and replied, "You can call it Hell for all I care." And so they did.

Hell, Michigan, plays up its name with attractions like the Creamatory ice-cream shop at Screams from Hell, where you can send postcards from Hell.

And it's been Hell ever since, though Colone says some of the towns-folk had to create a homeowner's association some years back to prevent the name from being changed to the more sedate Highland Lake. Hell runs for less than a mile on either side of a bend in Patterson Lake Road. The town, such as it is, is divided into what residents call Uptown (a barbecue joint that's being redeveloped), Midtown (the general store), and Downtown (the saloon).

Hi, From Hell

There are only three places in the world where people can say they officially live in Hell, plus a natural area named Hell on Grand Cayman (see page 136) that has a post office but no residents:

HELL, MICHIGAN: This small town outside Detroit has been Hell since 1841, when it was home to a general store and whiskey distillery.

HELL, NETHERLANDS: It's not clear how this farming village in the Dutch province of Gelderland came to be called Hell, but it may have originated from the word *helle,* meaning "a low-lying place." This Hell is mostly farmland, so you'll likely just make a quick stop for a selfie as proof you've been to Hell. The bigger nearby town of Nijkerk has restaurants and cafés.

HELL, NORWAY: The northernmost Hell may have gotten its name from the Old Norse word *hellir,* a reference to the overhanging cliffs in the area. Temperatures in this Hell can plummet to minus 13°F (−25°C) in winter. The two biggest attractions in the tiny town are the most photographed train station sign in Norway and an annual blues festival, called Blues in Hell.

Colone owns Uptown and Midtown, and is often referred to as the mayor of Hell, or as the town's owner. He's a genial guy, a gentle soul with an uncanny knack for puns and a love of the community he grew up in. In other words, he's the perfect guardian of Hell. He made the town what it is today after retiring from running a Chrysler dealership for 23 years.

His first order of business was to clean up Hell. It had gotten a little seedy, having become a place for bikers to party and, well, raise a little hell. So Colone bought Uptown and Midtown and came up with ways to market Hell as a stopping point for families on road trips, couples looking for a fun weekend destination, or the merely curious who get a kick out of a good pun.

Now the general store holds not only an impressive assortment of hell-themed paraphernalia, but also the Creamatory ice cream shop and a post office where you can send postcards—or just about anything else—postmarked from Hell. They'll even singe the edges with a lighter for that authentic straight-from-hell look. (Divorce papers are a popular item to mail from Hell, says Yvonne Williams, known as Reverend Vonn, who officiates weddings at Hell's Chapel of Love as "Hell's minister.")

Each year, thousands of tourists visit from all over the world, stopping in Hell Saloon for a beer and a "Hell of a BLT," or grabbing a T-shirt proclaiming "I've been to Hell and back." They also come for the wedding chapel, Screams putt-putt, and a scattering yard where you can make sure your loved ones' ashes end up in Hell. At the gift shop (or online), you can also pay to be mayor of Hell for a day or to own a square inch of Hell (the price has gone up from $9.99 to $13.33; Hell has inflation, too).

It turns out, Hell is also a nice place for a festival. October is a great time to visit, with Halloween-themed events all month, including a hearse show, a witches' wine night at the saloon, and a family-friendly festival with pumpkin carving and costumes. Or stop off to see the Grinch for Christmas pictures in December. For the Hell-O Summer Fest, dozens of vendors set up booths selling all manner of festival arts and crafts—some with a spooky twist, from extremely lifelike (or dead-like?) silicone body parts to just about anything you could want with a skull on it. You'll also find a DJ who's guaranteed to play "Monster Mash" more than once, slushies made with the local Michigan soda pop Faygo,

Kids can pose as little devils in Hell, which is meant to be a family-friendly destination. That's in large part thanks to its unofficial mayor, John Colone, who is responsible for the town's many devilish puns.

and plenty of motorcyclists who've made Hell a popular stop on rides through the lake region.

Weddings at Hell's Chapel tend to be fun for onlookers, too. At the 2023 summer festival, which I attended, Tricia Korade and Chris Edwards of Johnson City, Tennessee, professed true love in a "fake wedding" ceremony. The couple went all-out on the heaven-and-hell theme, with halos and devil horns perched on guests' heads. It was a sight to behold.

All in all, Hell makes for a surprisingly nice family getaway. It's located on Hell Creek, which runs through the Pinckney State Recreation Area, an 11,000-acre (4,450 ha) state park popular for biking, hiking, and fishing. It has plenty of vacation cottages and a lakefront beach where groups gather with coolers and grills. So sure, you could say that Hell is full of tourists and pitchfork-themed kitsch—but it's still a helluva good time.

Hell

A patch of black, spiky ground resembles the floor of hell.

This Hell is a prickly one. Here, jagged black spines poke out of the lush surroundings of the West Bay district of Grand Cayman, forming a landscape that looks designed to torture shoeless souls for eternity.

The sinister-looking limestone formations give the place its name, though who first came up with it is not clear exactly. Some say Hell was named by locals who thought it looked like the devil's lair, which is certainly plausible given that one can easily imagine demons hiding amid the menacing spikes. However, according to another story, the name stuck after a British general attempted hunting in the area, missed a shot at a bird, and bellowed, "Oh, hell!" (If that last one's true, it's not only the lamest origin story ever, but it also suggests that there should be a lot more hunting grounds named Hell.)

However it got its name, this particular Hell is a small one, about the size of a soccer field. Because of the black color of the rock formations, some visitors assume they're looking at a lava field. In reality, the

The small area designated as Hell on Grand Cayman
embraces its name with devil statues, gift shops, and postmarks from Hell.

spines are rocks made of what geologists call phytokarst, a landform
shaped by a special type of erosion involving algae.

These stringy life-forms (technically known as filamentous algae)
bore into the limestone and dissolve the calcite crystals found inside,
creating a delicate spongy texture. Their biological activity also results
in a black coating on the surface of the limestone, which would otherwise be white.

The blackened formations that give Hell its name are found just
above the high-tide line, where spray and mist from nearby breaking
waves sustain the algae.

The unusual black limestone formations that give Hell its name
are formed by algae.

Visitors to Hell can see the geologic feature for free, though be
aware: You can't walk on the spikes (nor would you want to; they're
pretty sharp). While you view the formation from platforms, make
sure to look for the carved statues of devils posed around the site, then
visit the three nearby gift shops and Hell post office, where you can
buy Hell-themed accoutrements including—what else?—postcards
from Hell.

The World's Rare Lakes of Fire

From the Ethiopian desert to Pacific islands and Antarctica, lava lakes are an elusive sight.

Lava lakes happen to be the best places to look, paraphrasing Johnny Cash, down, down, down into a burnin' ring of fire. These pools of molten lava form in the craters of slowly erupting volcanoes. They're the rarest of all volcanic features, forming only when lava burbles into a volcano's crater at just the right pace to keep itself hot and avoid solidifying—but not so fast that it spills out of the crater.

Even when conditions are right, most lava lakes are transient beasts. In recent years, only eight volcanoes have held lava lakes—and they tend to come and go without warning. To see one, you'll need to make sure that it still exists by the time you want to visit. Check with the park system associated with your lava lake of choice, or look it up on the Smithsonian's Global Volcanism Program website. The program collects data on volcanoes monitored around the world; many of the most active ones are updated on a weekly basis.

Many of them are true bucket-list destinations: remote, difficult to reach, and dangerous. But if you're still undaunted, here are nine best bets to catch a lava lake while it's still roiling:

Kīlauea, Hawaii: The Halemaʻumaʻu crater in Kīlauea has been home to a lava lake for most of the past several decades. It vanished in a 2018

Only eight volcanoes have persistent lava lakes. Most lava lakes are fleeting, because the molten rock from an eruption quickly cools and hardens.

eruption, then rushed back in 2020 to a lava lake more than 500 feet deep (150 m). Because Kīlauea's lava lake has been remarkably stable over time, scientists have used it as a portal to study the underworld of magma and to understand the forces that cause eruptions. It's also the easiest lava lake to see for yourself, by far. Visitors to Hawaiʻi Volcanoes National Park can see the summit lava lake filling Halemaʻumaʻu crater from public viewing areas in the park.

Erta Ale, Ethiopia: Another lava lake that has been active for decades is at Erta Ale, an active shield volcano (called this because of its low profile, like a shield lying on the ground) in the Danakil Depression (see page 197) in northeastern Ethiopia. Called the "smoking mountain," Erta Ale checks several boxes on a hell tour of the planet: It's in one of the hottest places on Earth and often has two lava lakes. No wonder it's also been called a "gateway to hell." Though it's not the easiest travel destination, adventure tour groups offer trips to the volcano lakes, and it's possible to drive within a few miles of the volcano.

Nyiragongo, Democratic Republic of the Congo: This classically cone-shaped volcano is considered one of the most dangerous in Africa, erupting constantly and sometimes violently, as it did in May 2021, when its lava flows stopped just short of the nearby city of Goma. The lava lake in its crater has been active since at least 1971, when monitoring began. Visitors to Virunga National Park can hire guides to lead the four- to six-hour hike to the top of Nyiragongo to see the lava lakes.

Villarrica, Chile: One of Chile's most active volcanoes, Villarrica often sports a beautiful but deadly whitecap of snow. The snow's runoff, mixed together with rainfall and glaciers, doesn't play nice with lava from frequent eruptions. The result: massive flows of debris and mud called lahars. The volcano has an intermittent lava lake, and occasionally releases large fountains of lava. Several adventure tour groups offer guided ascent of the mountain, but it's intended for experienced hikers and climbers, as the climb to the volcano's glacier requires using crampons.

Masaya, Nicaragua: This volcano in Nicaragua's largest national park is home to one of the world's most persistent lava lakes (see page 103). Masaya has disappeared and reappeared several times since Spanish explorers first recorded it in the 1500s but has mostly been present in recent decades. Various hiking routes are available in Masaya Volcano National Park, and they are less challenging than some of the other lava lake destinations.

Ambrym (Mount Marum), Vanuatu: The lake of fire that periodically crowns this volcano has been described as one of the world's most infernal sights. Neighboring Mount Benbow also held a lava lake, offering hikers the unique opportunity to witness two active lava lakes from one spot. Unfortunately, both lava lakes drained at the same time in late

2018, disappearing into a fissure created by an eruption. It's unknown when or if they will re-form.

Mount Erebus, Antarctica: Earth's southernmost active volcano sits on Ross Island in Antarctica and has held a lava lake since at least the early 1970s, when it was discovered. At nearly 12,500 feet high (3,800 m), Erebus is a serious climb, and dangerous—it often flings huge chunks of molten rock that can explode on landing.

Mount Michael, South Sandwich Islands: The world's most recently discovered lava lake was found in 2022 on remote Saunders Island in the southern Atlantic, about 1,000 miles (1,610 km) off the coast of Antarctica in the storm-tossed South Sandwich Islands. More people have been to the moon than to the top of Mount Michael. So if you're dead set on going, you'll need to find your way onto a scientific expedition—or, if you're wealthy enough, fund one yourself!

BEFORE YOU GO

To find out if a volcano is erupting or holds a lava lake, go to the Smithsonian Institution's Global Volcanism Program website, then navigate to their database and use the "volcano search" feature to find a volcano by name.

Phlegraean Fields

The famed "burning fields" inspired Dante's interpretation of hell.

W hen driving through Italy's Campania region, it's easy to be lulled into a sense of peace and tranquility, even as you cruise atop an active volcano. Orange and lemon groves dot a rolling green landscape that ends at the sea with views of the island paradise of Ischia. Once you've climbed a hill and rounded a turn, a volcanic crater heaves into sudden view. It's a breathtaking sight: Blue waters and skies frame a pale, fuming gash in the earth: the Solfatara di Pozzuoli.

This ancient crater northwest of Naples is rich in both volcanic activity and underworld lore. Known as the Phlegraean Fields (or Campi Flegrei, meaning "burning fields"), it's one of the most famous geothermal areas in history, featuring in myth and legend for thousands of years, including helping to inspire the landscape of Dante's *Inferno*. And its story isn't over; experts say it could erupt again anytime.

The Phlegraean Fields is an eight-mile-wide (13 km) area of volcanic features extending from the town of Pozzuoli into the Gulf of Pozzuoli. Connecting all these features belowground is a supervolcano, a volcanic center so large that it's capable of the highest-magnitude eruptions known to science. The fields today are what's left over from an eruption of this supervolcano nearly 40,000 years ago, a blast that ejected so much magma that the volcano collapsed in on itself and left behind a cratered landscape pockmarked with steaming hot springs and fumaroles that exhale hot steam and sulfurous gas.

The Solfatara di Pozzuoli is one of the Phlegraean Fields' largest volcanic features. A solfatara (meaning "sulfur place") is a large fumarole that emits sulfurous compounds. This one formed around 4,000 years ago. In Roman times, it was known as the home of Vulcan, the god of fire. Later accounts name it as the place of beheadings for early Christian martyrs, including San Gennaro, who became the patron saint of Naples (see page 147).

The volcanically active Phlegraean Fields region has long fascinated scientists, scholars, and artists. Here, Sicilian royalty observe a 1771 eruption.

The Phlegraean Fields haven't had a significant eruption since 1538, but that doesn't mean there's no activity. Its bubbling mud pools and fumaroles are still hazards. The area is constantly monitored for volcanic activity, a grave concern for the three million or so people who live in Naples and the surrounding areas.

The Solfatara used to be open to visitors, with walking paths framed by low wooden fences winding through the crater. But in 2017, an 11-year-old boy died when a piece of the crater floor crumbled beneath his feet. Compounding the tragedy, both his parents died trying to rescue him, leaving his seven-year-old brother behind. The horrific incident forced closure of the crater floor to tourists and spawned a long-running lawsuit over liability.

Today, the crater can only be viewed from the road above. Remnants of the wooden fences that once guided visitors still traverse the chalky white crater floor, and steam billows up the surrounding hillsides. It's an eerie and otherworldly sight.

Other signs of the region's volcanic activity are scattered around Pozzuoli. On marble columns at an ancient Roman market called the Macellum of Pozzuoli, for instance, you can see boreholes created by marine mollusks 20 feet (6 m) up the columns, evidence that the land there at some point sank below sea level and later raised back up (a geological phenomenon called bradyseism, in which land shifts as underground magma chambers fill and empty). And just a few miles west of the Solfatara, you can see Monte Nuovo ("New Mountain"), a volcanic cinder cone more than 400 feet (120 m) tall created by a massive eruption in 1538.

🔱 BEFORE YOU GO

For the best viewing of the Solfatara di Pozzuoli, pull off the Coste d'Agnano road at the highest point of the hill.

Naples

Explore a city deeply connected to visions of heaven, hell, and purgatory.

n Naples, ancient history blends seamlessly with the present, and the bonds between living and dead remain tight. You can stroll past ancient Greek ruins in the Piazza Bellini, dip underground to see Roman-era shops under the city's streets, then catch a Catholic Mass at the Duomo. And for travelers interested in the afterlife, Naples has it all. Within a short drive, you can visit the ancient Greek entrance to Hades (see Phlegraean Fields, page 144), monuments to heaven, and a church dedicated to souls in purgatory.

The 2,500-year-old city lies tucked between Mount Vesuvius and the volcanically active Phlegraean Fields (or Campi Flegrei)—a perfect place to inspire a writer's vision of a flaming, steaming hell. And in the 1300s, Dante Alighieri did just that, vividly describing the underworld and its occupants in *Inferno,* the first part of his masterpiece, *Divine Comedy*.

An underworld tour of Naples properly begins with paying respects to the Roman poet Virgil at his tomb in a quiet park at the city's southern end. Then, you can tip your hat to Dante, who followed Virgil centuries later in describing the underworld. An imposing 19th-century statue of him looms over Piazza Dante, a large public square with an entrance to the metro in the city's historic center.

From Piazza Dante, it's a short walk through the city's narrow cobblestone streets to a skull-filled church where generations of Neapolitans have communed with the dead—specifically, with souls in purgatory. Santa Maria delle Anime del Purgatorio ad Arco was consecrated in 1638 by a congregation dedicated to praying for souls in purgatory. In particular, the faithful prayed for those who hadn't received proper burial rites, including many who died of plague and were buried in a mass grave under the church. These unfortunate souls were believed to be trapped in purgatory, where they would be punished for their sins before going to heaven. The church's faithful believed they could help trapped souls move on to heaven through prayer.

The church was built with two levels: a main level that represents the earthly world and a lower level intended as a journey into purgatory. The church itself is richly decorated with skull-and-bone carvings and artwork that depicts souls in purgatory, while the lower level holds the hypogeum, an underground tomb with niches in the stone walls, something like cubbyholes, holding human skulls and other bones. Pits were also dug into the floor to hold mass graves.

After World War II left many Neapolitans mourning missing relatives, people began to "adopt" particular skulls from the niches of the church's underground crypt in their stead. In particular, elderly women and widows would polish and dote on their chosen skull and pray fervently for its owner's soul. In exchange, they would ask for protection or favors from the dead (which might come in the form of marital help or, sometimes, winning lottery numbers).

Practitioners became known as the Neapolitan Cult of the Dead, or Skull Cult, not because they were worshipping skulls or the dead—

The Purgatorio ad Arco church is filled with imagery of skulls and skeletons, signs of the congregation's devotion to these relics and the souls of the dead.

they believed they were acting in accordance with Catholic doctrine—but because of their intense attachment to mortal remains.

Today, the Purgatorio ad Arco is open to the public, and for a small entrance fee visitors can see both levels of the church, including the remaining skulls in the hypogeum (many were moved to Naples's Fontanelle cemetery in the 1990s). The most famous among these relics is the skull known as Princess Lucia, or the "virgin bride," adorned with a crown and veil and still seen as a patron to young brides today.

The Catholic Church banned the cult in 1969, but the devoted continue to commune with the dead at the church. Some bring mementos and laminated photographs of dead loved ones to pray for, and some, it is said, still keep the Neapolitan Skull Cult alive.

If you're in need of a lift in mood after visiting the Purgatorio ad Arco, just walk a few blocks to the Sansevero Chapel Museum (or Cappella Sansevero), a monument to heaven built, incongruously, by a prince with a diabolical reputation. Raimondo di Sangro, Prince of Sansevero, was an inventor, alchemist, and Freemason in the 18th-century kingdom of Naples. In the 1740s, he began renovating the chapel adjacent to his family's palace, and the work became an obsession, his goal to build a majestic temple lavishly decorated with the finest marble sculptures and works of art. These include statues representing the virtues, an enormous ceiling fresco of heaven, and the remarkable "Veiled Christ," a marble statue whose ethereal carved "veil" is so realistic that legend long held it was created from real cloth and turned to stone using a magical petrifying potion.

Because di Sangro practiced alchemy and was a member of the secret society of the Freemasons, also banned by the Catholic Church, he was the subject of many dark rumors, including that he had created the potion used on the "Veiled Christ." Worse, some believed that he had people killed to use their body parts in strange experiments and inventions. It didn't help that one of his hobbies was creating what he called anatomical machines: detailed models of the human circulatory system supported on real human skeletons.

Today, visitors can see two of these anatomical machines (don't worry, research shows the blood vessels are made of wax, silk, and wire) as well as the impressive collection of religious art that di Sangro commissioned for his family chapel.

Tens of thousands of skulls are stacked in the catacombs of the Cimitero delle Fontanelle, including many venerated by the Neapolitan Skull Cult.

To get a fuller sense of Naples's connection to death, it's also worth a visit to the Catacombs of San Gennaro. The catacombs were an important burial site for early Christians and, for a time, held the remains of San Gennaro (St. Januarius), the patron saint of Naples. According to local legend, San Gennaro was martyred in the fourth century by beheading at the Solfatara di Pozzuoli (see page 145), a steaming volcanic crater in the Phlegraean Fields and the same place where Dante was inspired by visions of hell a millennium later.

Today, San Gennaro is famous for his "blood miracle." The saint's dried blood is held in a glass vial and brought out three times a year (in September, December, and May). On some of these occasions, San Gennaro is said to perform a miracle by turning the blood from solid to liquid; when this happens, it's seen as a good omen for the people of Naples. Likewise, when it fails to liquefy, it's a bad sign. This ritual has even been linked to Naples's geological activity; two months after the saint's blood failed to liquefy in September 1980, a massive earthquake struck southern Italy and killed more than 3,000 people. Neapolitans are quick to point this out if the miracle is questioned.

For travelers looking for a city full of mysteries and miracles, Naples is a perfect place to explore. Wind your way through its maze of narrow streets and you're sure to stumble across some surprises.

🔱 BEFORE YOU GO

To expand your visit to Naples and get more context for the area's history, you can also visit the National Archaeological Museum of Naples. The archaeological museum takes visitors through thousands of years of the region's history and holds a large collection of artifacts from the towns of Pompeii and Herculaneum, both destroyed by the eruption of Mount Vesuvius in A.D. 79 (see page 155).

Dante's *Inferno*

One of the most vivid portrayals ever of Christian hell was written in the 14th century by Dante Alighieri, an Italian poet. Dante's *Inferno* is the first part of his three-part epic poem *Divine Comedy*, which also includes *Purgatorio* (purgatory) and *Paradiso* (heaven).

Inferno is written as a first-person account of a fictional descent into nine circles of hell, guided by the soul of the long-dead Roman poet Virgil (who Dante idolized). To get to Dante's hell, a ferryman called Charon shuttles souls across the Acheron River (see page 29)—the same journey the ancient Greeks described to get to Hades. Dante's hell is a path that spirals into the depths of the earth, with each circle containing sinners of a different sort:

FIRST CIRCLE: Here, Dante finds the souls of those whose only sin was not being Christian. Upstanding citizens of pre-Christian yore such as Homer, Socrates, and Hippocrates live here in a castle where they can debate one another for eternity.

SECOND CIRCLE: Things heat up a bit in the next circle, home to those guilty of lust, including famous adulterers such as Cleopatra. Their eternal punishment is a windstorm that blows them ceaselessly to and fro, representing their restless hearts.

THIRD CIRCLE: In the circle of gluttony, those who overindulged must flail forever in a filthy pool while being bombarded with a cold and stinking rain. The three-headed beast Cerberus makes sure they suffer, barking incessantly and clawing at the spirits.

FOURTH CIRCLE: In the circle of greed, hoarders and spendthrifts face off against one another in an eternal contest shoving boulders back and forth, a task as never-ending as the accumulation of wealth.

FIFTH CIRCLE: The River Styx runs through the fifth circle of hell, creating a foul marsh where those who were wrathful fight one another in the muck. Those who were merely sullen and surly are stuck gurgling in the sludge beneath the water's surface.

SIXTH CIRCLE: For their offense against God, heretics (those who believe the body has no soul) spend eternity encased in flaming tombs. Here, Dante finds Epicurus, the Greek philosopher who believed that there is nothing after death and that humans' highest goal is to pursue the pleasures of life.

SEVENTH CIRCLE: At this level of hell, we get to the murderers. The seventh circle is split into three rings, with killers occupying the outer ring (a river of flames and boiling blood), people who died by suicide in the middle (where they're turned into trees and fed upon by monsters), and blasphemers in the inner ring's fiery wasteland.

EIGHTH CIRCLE: Known as Malebolge, roughly meaning "evil ditches," the eighth circle is made of eight ditches, each piled with the deceitful in their various forms—seducers, flatterers, false prophets, thieves, hypocrites, and more.

NINTH CIRCLE: In the final circle, history's three greatest traitors—Judas Iscariot, the apostle who betrayed Jesus, along with Brutus and Cassius, who murdered Julius Caesar—are frozen in an icy lake. Satan himself is frozen waist-deep here, gnashing at the sinners with his three mouths.

ITALY

Pompeii and Herculaneum

**Mount Vesuvius brought the wrath of hell
to these once thriving towns.**

f ever hell came to Earth, it came on an October day in A.D. 79 when Mount Vesuvius destroyed the cities of Pompeii and Herculaneum in one fiery stroke.

Roman author Pliny the Elder and his nephew, 18-year-old Pliny the Younger, witnessed the eruption from across the Bay of Naples and compared the ominous cloud rising in the distance to the broad-topped umbrella pine trees that today's tourists still walk beneath in the shadow of Vesuvius. Today, we call it a mushroom cloud. The eruption shot superheated gas and rock 21 miles (34 km) into the air, releasing 100,000 times the energy of the Hiroshima atomic bomb.

In the early hours of the eruption, people scrambled to flee. Many of Pompeii's 20,000 or so residents did make it out; those left behind were enslaved people and others with no means of quick escape. Those poor souls suffocated in a cloud of toxic gas that hung over for three days as hot ash and pumice rained down until the city was completely buried.

The neighboring town of Herculaneum came to an even more horrific end. Herculaneum was a seaside resort for the wealthy—think of

an ancient Roman version of Martha's Vineyard. Many of its 5,000 residents lived there only in the summer, escaping sweltering Rome for luxurious vacation villas. Perhaps that's why there weren't very many people in Herculaneum when Vesuvius erupted in October.

But for those who remained—servants and workers, and some lingering vacationers—that day was a fiery torment. Herculaneum was much closer to Vesuvius, and its residents didn't have the luxury of an incoming cloud of ash and debris to warn them, as those in Pompeii had. Instead, the people of Herculaneum heard the volcano's initial eruption, and many tried to flee, only for Vesuvius to belch out a surge of superheated gas and ash, known as a pyroclastic flow, that raced straight toward the town at more than 932°F (500°C). A human body is no match for that. When scientists analyzed the skeletonized remains of 80 people who had taken refuge in boat chambers along the beach in Herculaneum, they found that the victims had died in a fraction of a second, before they even had time to react in self-defense; their blood boiled, their clothing and flesh vaporized, and their hands and feet were left flexed by the contraction of seared muscle. The heat was so intense that one victim's brain was even found vitrified, or turned to glass, inside his skull.

As horrible as that is, those who died immediately were the lucky ones, because the entire town was then buried in lava. Even today, only a few square blocks of Herculaneum have been laboriously chipped out of the hardened lava rock that entombed the city.

The labors of archaeologists have uncovered a vivid picture of the horror of that day. One of the first things visitors see as they enter Herculaneum is a set of skeletons huddled under arches along the city walls.

"The Great Eruption of Mt. Vesuvius" by Louis-Jean Desprez imagines the desperate attempt to flee Pompeii during the A.D. 79 eruption.

These are the remains of those who rushed down Herculaneum's main road, trying unsuccessfully to reach the beach and escape by boat.

For more than a thousand years, Pompeii and Herculaneum lay buried under tons of ash, pumice, and lava. Eventually, people forgot the towns ever existed. So imagine the public's surprise in 1738 when archaeologists began uncovering the entire lost city of Herculaneum. In 1748, work began at Pompeii and has continued off and on to the present day.

Now, visitors wander the streets of both towns. At Herculaneum, only a small number of homes have been excavated, but they're far more complete than what you'll see in Pompeii. They're filled with colorful frescoes and detailed mosaics, truly giving a sense of the wealth and luxury their inhabitants enjoyed before the eruption.

Most of Pompeii, on the other hand, has been excavated. It takes hours to traverse its streets, walking mostly past foundations and low crumbled walls. Then there are the human remains, preserved by fine ash that covered them and calcified over time to create a kind of protective shell. More than 1,000 victims have been found in the ash of Pompeii. Many of the bodies (or plaster casts of the delicate remains) are now in museums, but one of the most famous remains in the city.

Encased in a glass box, the ashen figure of a young woman looks almost as if she's been sculpted from stone. This body, and others in Pompeii, are actually plaster casts made in the 1800s by Giuseppe Fiorelli, an enterprising archaeologist who discovered that the shapes of victims' bodies had been preserved in the hardened ash long after the bodies within had decomposed. By pouring plaster into the remaining voids, Fiorelli was able to capture remarkable details of the bodies, even hair and clothing. The young woman identified as Victim No. 10 lay prone, the curve of her belly revealing her to be pregnant, her forearm thrust under her face as though she tried to shield herself from the

Plaster casts at Pompeii's Garden of the Fugitives preserve the remains of
Pompeians in the positions in which they fell as the eruption overcame them.

ash and gases that ultimately suffocated her. In the Garden of the Fugitives at the edge of Pompeii, 13 more victims—children and adults—
were found in a vineyard, where they appeared to be trying to escape
the city. Plaster casts of their remains are displayed at the site as well,
the bodies frozen as they were when they died.

That hellish day forever changed the entire landscape around
Mount Vesuvius. Before the eruption, the mountain had a pointed peak.
Today, Vesuvius, as seen from Pompeii and Herculaneum, has two
broad humps, with a missing chunk in the middle where the peak used

to be. It's a reminder of not only Earth's powerful forces, but also of how quickly those forces can overcome us.

Because, as geologists have warned, Vesuvius will erupt again. It's impossible to predict when the next blast will come, they say, but it could be any time. And it could be much bigger than the one that destroyed Pompeii and Herculaneum. More than a million people now live in Naples alone, and a major eruption could affect as many as three million.

Today, tourists can walk the streets of Pompeii in the shadow of Mount Vesuvius, which remains one of the world's most dangerous active volcanoes.

Deadvlei (Dead Valley)

One of the planet's most beautiful hellscapes
is found in its oldest desert.

With its ghostly white floor and lifeless desert landscape—too dry for the dead trees stranded here to even decompose—Namibia's Deadvlei is a vision of a hot, thirsty hell.

This is one of the bleakest landscapes on Earth, yet also one of the most striking: The starkness of sun-blackened trees rising from white salt-clay pans is framed by the intense colors of blue desert skies and towering pink-orange sand dunes. At night, starry skies provide an even more magical backdrop. However, visitors do have to contend with the extreme climate. Much like the varied levels of Dante's imagined hell, Deadvlei's temperatures range from near-freezing winter nights to blazing summer days reaching 105°F (40°C).

Deadvlei (or Dead Valley) is found in the Namib Desert along Namibia's Atlantic coast. Desert landscapes shift with changing climates, but the Namib has stuck around the longest, making it the world's oldest desert. Deep within its parched landscape, the Namib-Naukluft National Park protects a vast area of more than 19,000 square miles (50,000 km²), about double the size of Vermont. Within the park are a number of salt-clay pans surrounded by dunes, including Deadvlei and its better-known neighbor, Sossusvlei, which features towering sand dunes in shades of orange.

In the local Nama language, *sossus* means "no return" and *vlei* means a "marsh or temporary lake," referring to the Tsauchab River that flows into the desert from the east and dries up before reaching the ocean. This river accounts for the stark white color of Deadvlei; when heavy rains swell the Tsauchab and create smaller ephemeral streams through the desert, water fills the clay pans. When the marshes dry up, salt is left behind, adding to the whiteness of Deadvlei's dry pans.

The blackened remains of long-dead camel thorn trees stand out against the white salt pans and sunset hues of Deadvlei (Dead Valley).

Though called the Dead Valley, there is life here. Look closely and you may see the tracks of the small rodents, reptiles, and arthropods that make the desert home. Many are unique to the Namib, including the aptly named fog beetles that survive the dry climate by collecting morning fog on bumps lining their backs. And in wetter times, larger animals like antelope and ostriches venture into the desert.

The blackened remains of dead camel thorn trees scattered through Dead Valley hint at less brutal times in the desert's past. Around 900 years ago, the combination of a drying climate and shifting dunes cut the area off from the Tsauchab River. Without the water source, the camel thorn trees in Dead Valley all died. Unable to decompose in the extremely dry climate, the trees simply stood in the scorching sun for centuries like dark sentinels of death.

Today, Dead Valley and especially its neighbor Sossusvlei are major draws for tourism in Namibia. Lodges cater to visitors at every price point, from luxury villas with private plunge pools to eco-friendly campsites that provide the desert basics of shade, water, and incredible views.

Visitors can explore the park by safari flight, hot-air balloon, horseback, or on foot. For those on foot, the edge of Dead Valley offers the chance to photograph, or even climb, an enormous dune known as Big Daddy. At about 1,066 feet high (325 m), or nearly the height of the Empire State Building, it's one of the tallest sand dunes in the world. The top of the dune offers amazing views of Deadvlei and bragging rights—trekking in the soft sand is described as strenuous and slow.

For those who take it on, Deadvlei rewards with the otherworldly beauty of a hell on Earth.

Dead Sea

Hot, smelly, and super salty—the Dead Sea has all the elements of a briny hell.

For thousands of years, people have been trying to describe the Dead Sea's indescribable landscape with various names. The oldest is the Salt Sea, or Yam Ha-Melakh, but it's also been called the Stinking Lake, Lake Asphaltites, the Devil's Sea, and even the Mouth of Hell.

Most of these names aptly capture some aspect of the Dead Sea: Parts of the lakeshore do indeed stink thanks to sulfur deposits; it does spit up asphalt (occasionally in chunks the size of a school bus); and it is certainly salty. But why link it to hell?

Perhaps dark rumors got started because the spot seems so strange and hostile to life. With a salinity of about 34 percent, the Dead Sea is about 10 times as salty as the ocean and ranks as one of the world's saltiest bodies of water. Its salinity comes from its position below sea level in an arid, nearly barren landscape. The sea gets all its water from the Jordan River, and as the incoming water evaporates in the hot desert basin, the salt it carries is left behind. For at least 15,000 years, that salt has been accumulating.

People are still amazed when they float like fishing bobbers in the Dead Sea's salty waters, and this phenomenon must have seemed

The Dead Sea is so saline that salt crystals precipitate out of the water and create large, intricate salt formations.

bizarre, even supernatural, to ancient people. Adding to the hellish effect, the Dead Sea is in a desert where air temperatures regularly reach into the 100s in Fahrenheit (40s in Celsius) and the water stays warm even in the winter.

Or maybe it's the region's history: Biblical scholars have long believed the wicked cities of Sodom and Gomorrah were buried under the Dead Sea after God rained down fire and brimstone to destroy them. The Dead Sea never quite shook off the bad reputation.

There were rumors that iron would float on the Dead Sea's surface, but feathers would sink. That birds could not fly over it without dying and falling from the sky (an avian hazard also linked to Lake Avernus in Italy, see page 46). Reports claimed that the lake emitted foul and noxious vapors, or that it constantly smoked like the fires of hell. One 14th-century Christian pilgrim even reported that if you picked up beautiful pebbles found on its shores, your hand would stink to high heaven for three days.

Such tales of the Dead Sea fascinated medieval Christians, especially, and it became an important pilgrimage site. Many of the accounts were exaggerations, however, if not pure fancy.

In reality, the Dead Sea is both a hellish and a beautiful place. Yes, it's hot, harsh, and inhospitable. It's so salty (containing mostly potassium chloride) that plants and animals cannot live in its waters. But it does hold an abundance of salt-loving microbes, and many people find it achingly beautiful, especially as the surrounding Moab mountains take on different colors throughout the day—pink-washed in morning light, cobalt and sparkling under full sun, and pastel hues as the sun sets.

The Hells of Beppu

**Superhot hot springs fill this town
with steamy surprises.**

The hilly Japanese city of Beppu is a paradise of hells. That may sound strange, until you learn that the locals refer to some of their hottest hot springs as *jigoku*—translation, "hell." This small resort town on Japan's southern island of Kyushu is home to around 2,300 hot springs—the second most in the world behind Yellowstone National Park (see page 193). All over town, plumes of steam rise from pools of water, creating a mysterious and otherworldly environment worth getting lost in.

According to local lore, a Buddhist monk named Ippen Shōnin tamed the once scorching hells of Beppu through prayer, allowing everyone since to enjoy them. And so, many of Beppu's hot springs are used as onsen, traditional Japanese baths and inns built around natural hot springs. But its most famous steamy sights are the hells, which are huge tourist attractions even though they're too hot for bathing.

The seven most popular hot springs in Beppu are known together as the Jigoku Meguri, or "hell circuit," representing the hot hells of Jigoku, the multileveled hell of Japanese Buddhism (see page 88). Each hot spring has its charms, but the most hellish—Chinoike Jigoku, or the Blood Pond Hell—is a crimson-colored pool presided over by a collection of sculpted demons, some carved into the surrounding rocks.

Chinoike Jigoku's blood-red color comes from natural iron oxide deposits on the pond bed. The water is hellishly hot, reaching a scalding 172°F (78°C) that makes it too hot for bathing—but you can dip your feet in a prepared foot bath that's been cooled to more bearable temperatures. Or test out the purported healing powers of hell-pond mud with skin creams sold at the site, which have long been used to soften and soothe skin conditions like psoriasis and eczema. Then sample dumplings and other bites at the site's Gokurakutei restaurant specializing in *jigoku mushi,* or "hell steaming," in which containers of food are steamed right in the hot spring.

The nighttime cityscape of Beppu, Japan, is punctuated by steam rising from some of its more than 2,000 hot springs.

Each of the other hells on the circuit is its own steamy treat:

Sea Hell is Beppu's biggest hell and features a spacious garden with walking paths. The large, steamy pond is a beautiful pale blue thanks to high levels of iron sulfate. A smaller pond has reddish waters.

Shaved Head Hell is full of thick gray mud that forms domes as the hot spring bubbles up. The large bubbles are said to look like the shaved head of a monk.

Spouting Hell (or Tornado Hell) has a boiling hot geyser that goes off about every half hour.

Cooking Pot Hell is composed of multiple pools overseen by a devil statue posing as a chef. The site offers the opportunity to try more snacks, such as eggs, cooked via hell steaming.

White Pond Hell is a milky white color due to high concentrations of minerals in the water.

Monster Mountain Hell reaches water temperatures near boiling and has fenced-off pools of less-hot water that hold nearly 100 captive crocodiles.

⚕ BEFORE YOU GO

Five of the hells of Beppu are located near one another in the Kannawa district, and two are in the Shibaseki district. Bus tours visit all seven of them in about two and a half hours, or you can visit each site individually.

Blood Falls

If hell froze over, it might look like this.

Imagine a frigid, desolate place where a towering blood-red waterfall oozes from the ice. Hell, right? Well, that's exactly the gruesome sight geologist Griffith Taylor discovered during an expedition to Antarctica in 1911.

It must have been a shock to see: a curtain of red at the tip of a massive glacier—later named Taylor Glacier, for the explorer—cascading onto an ice-covered lake. Even more eerie, the red water was *moving*. How could any liquid flow in this completely frozen environment?

The cascade was aptly named Blood Falls, and for the next century its gory color remained a mystery. In 2017, scientists finally discovered that a complex network of rivers lies beneath the glacier. These rivers are filled with iron-rich brine, which turns red when exposed to oxygen and gives Blood Falls its crimson hue.

The water feeding Blood Falls is highly unusual because it flows from an ancient source trapped underneath the glacier, rather than being constantly replenished by rain or snow. About two million years ago, during a warmer climate, the sea level was much higher than it is today. As the climate cooled and the glacier began to form, a pocket of seawater became trapped under the ice. The rivers' high salt content kept the trapped water from freezing solid. Salt water has a lower freez-

The blood-red water oozing from Taylor Glacier looks like something out of the ninth circle of hell in Dante's *Inferno*, where the devil is frozen in ice.

ing point than fresh water and actually releases heat as it freezes. That means the freezing brine actually works to melt some of the ice around it, creating the constant supply of red, running water.

Over thousands of years, iron from the rock below the glacier leached into the ancient water. Along with this salty water and iron, bacteria were trapped under the ice. The microbes have survived there ever since in a sort of time capsule frozen into one of Earth's most extreme environments. To do so, they adapted to the cold temperatures, extreme salinity, and high pressure found under the massive glacier, eking out a living using the sulfur and iron in the water.

Thanks to its unique geology, Blood Falls is the coldest glacier on Earth with flowing water. But to see it in person is a feat; you'll need to get to the Dry Valleys of East Antarctica. The only ways to do this are to travel by helicopter from either New Zealand's Scott Base, the U.S. McMurdo Station, or—more likely, for tourists—to take a cruise ship in the Ross Sea.

A Cold Day in Bloody Hell?

Most visions of hell tend toward the hot and fiery, but ice and cold have a place in the pantheon of hells, too. Both Buddhist tradition and Dante's *Inferno* speak of cold places and frozen levels of hell. In fact, Dante made the deepest level of hell one filled with ice, and then buried the devil in it up to his waist.

Another odd geological feature found in some versions of hell is the river of blood. Hindu texts speak of the Vaitarna River lying between Earth and Naraka, the infernal realm of the god of death, Yama. While the righteous see the river as filled with pure, sweet water, the sinful see a river of blood. Dante also wrote of a bloody river, the Phlegethon, that flows through the seventh circle of hell and cascades to the eighth.

Haw Par Villa

A theme park makes an unforgettable display of the 10 Courts of Hell.

Haw Par Villa is sometimes called a Buddhist amusement park—if you can imagine an amusement park set in hell. Another way to think of it is a combination quirky theme park, botanical garden, and Sunday school.

The large grounds are filled with koi ponds, walking paths, art exhibits—and a variety of macabre displays of horrors that await sinners in the underworld. One of the main features of the park is the 10 Courts of Hell, where you can walk through more than 1,000 statues and 150 kitschy life-size dioramas that were designed to explore how different cultures around the world see the afterlife and to teach morality lessons according to traditional Chinese values by illustrating in vivid detail the tortures meted out in hell to sinners of every ilk. It's a bit like visiting a roadside attraction in the United States with brightly colored dinosaur statues, except instead of *T. rex* fighting an *Allosaurus,* you'll see a demon statue cutting the head off a murderer.

Set in a cavelike maze with spooky lighting, the vivid re-creations of the 10 levels of hell operate as courts where the dead are judged and punished. The levels are specific to the sins committed, as are the punishments. In the fourth level, for instance, those who have been disloyal to their parents are ground under a large stone. A diorama depicts this in excruciating detail, with body parts sticking out from between the (painted) bloody stones.

The original Haw Par Villa was built in 1937 by entrepreneurs and brothers Aw Boon Haw and Aw Boon Par and was originally called Tiger Balm Gardens, named for an ointment that their family business manufactured. The Japanese bombed the villa during World War II, but the brothers continued to add hell-themed statues and dioramas to the gardens for years afterward. In 1954, the garden became a public park, and Haw Par Villa still remains free to the public, though the museum housing the most elaborate dioramas charges admission.

Elaborate dioramas at Haw Par Villa illustrate the tortures of hell and other Chinese mythology, such as the legend of the Eight Immortals pictured here.

18 Levels of Hell

Chinese hell has a long and storied history that mixes Taoism, Confucianism, Buddhism, and other folklore traditions into today's view of the underworld.

The influence of Buddhism in medieval China led to a version of hell called Diyu, in which people must cycle between death and rebirth. They are punished for their sins before reincarnation in an underworld that functions as a kind of purgatory. The most common vision of this purgatory is the 10 Courts of Hell. In each court, souls are judged and punishments meted out, from frigid ice caverns for burglars to volcanic streams for violent offenders. There's even an enormous mortar in which tax evaders are crushed with a spiked pestle.

However, the exact number of levels in hell varies across legends and time. In one variation, 18 levels of torment await sinners, each tailored to specific sins. Not only are the tortures in these 18 levels horrific, but they're also recurring. For example, once a soul has been, say, torn apart in one round of torture, its "body" is reconstituted so that it can be torn apart again and again.

The park was redeveloped and modernized in the 1980s, restoring statues and adding animatronics and performance spaces. During the 1970s and '80s, the park reported a million visitors a year. Since then, it has had to keep updating and reinventing itself to compete with newer attractions, but the goal remains the same: to show off Chinese folklore and mythology.

In 2020, the Hell's Museum complex opened, featuring the long-running 10 Courts of Hell as its centerpiece, plus dioramas illustrating scenes from classic Chinese literature and legends.

Rotorua

A town built on fire and brimstone is a strange and beautiful hell.

New Zealand's wild places are so dramatic and extreme that it can feel like heaven and hell have been swirled together into one topsy-turvy landscape. And nowhere embodies that more than the active volcanic zone surrounding the city of Rotorua.

Of the country's two main islands, North Island has the most volcanic activity—and the hell-themed destinations that go with it. In particular, Rotorua and the surrounding areas have some of the most gorgeously hellish places on Earth. Also known as "Sulphur City," this lakeside city of about 70,000 people boasts 500 pools fed by hot springs, seven active geysers, and bubbling mud pools in the heart of downtown. Also nearby is Mount Tarawera, an active volcano that's safe enough to climb (you can even scramble down the rocky scree walls into its caldera).

The city stretches along the southern shore of Lake Rotorua, which itself lies in a large volcanic crater formed by an eruption about 240,000 years ago. The first thing you'll notice in downtown Rotorua is the smell:

The city of Rotorua sits in an active volcanic zone amid fumaroles, hot springs, and geysers, like these in Whakarewarewa Thermal Village.

Soak your feet—or your whole body—in warm mud baths drawn from
the bubbling sulfurous mud springs of Rotorua.

A sulfurous odor reminiscent of rotten eggs wafts in on the breeze.
Depending on which way the wind is blowing, you can catch whiffs of
hydrogen sulfide all over town (the hills to the south offering the best
respite). But as the locals say, you get used to it pretty quickly.

A walk downtown through Rotorua's public parks gives a proper
introduction to life in an active geothermal area. In Kuirau Park, you
stroll through pleasant grassy lawns and pergolas, past park benches
and charming wooden bridges. But strangely, along the way you also
pass bubbling mud pools and steaming hot springs. Though they're
tucked behind wooden fences, they're so close you could touch them—if
that weren't a terrible idea, which it is.

It's an unusual park that has to warn visitors with signs like "Danger:
Burns and geothermal gas can be fatal." But it's worth visiting to see
how closely people here live with volcanic activity. Two geothermally
heated public footbaths in the park are great spots to stop and dip weary
feet after a day of traipsing through hell.

Likewise, the Sanatorium Reserve at Sulphur Point is a good place to grasp the lifestyle and history of this place. The reserve is a stretch of public lands along the rim of a peninsula jutting into the southern part of Lake Rotorua. The local Maori *iwi* (group of tribes) gifted 3,000 acres (1,214 ha) to the British Crown in 1880 to establish a town on Lake Rotorua with land for recreation, sanitoriums, hospitals, and other amenities. Since then, the site has hosted everything from a sulfur mine and rubbish dump to hot springs for bathing and sports fields.

Today, there's green space with ecological restoration projects to drive out invasive species (rats and opossums are particular problems), as well as a walkway through a geothermal area. You'll see steaming holes in the ground called fumaroles, hot mud pools, and boiling hot springs. Stay on the boardwalk to avoid the sulfur mounds; these crusty bumps in the ground can be hollow. Step on one and you might release dangerous geothermal gases.

Another popular tourist destination is the geothermal area and mud bath known as Hell's Gate. Like in Sulphur Point, visitors can walk on a protected boardwalk through land that steams with hot springs

Kuirau and the Taniwha

Maori legend holds that Lake Kuirau, the central feature of Rotorua's downtown Kuirau park, got its name from a beautiful young woman named Kuirau who used to swim in the lake. A large Taniwha—a supernatural being who lives in deep pools or caves— would watch her swim every day until he couldn't stand it and snatched her up. Kuirau was never seen again, and the gods were so angry they made the lake boil to rid it of the Taniwha. It boils and steams to this day.

Sulfur: Hell's Element

Biblical hell often includes evocative language of fire and brimstone. But what, exactly, is brimstone? If you picture something like burning rocks, you're not far off; brimstone is actually just another word for sulfur.

Sulfur is literally an element of the underworld, found in vast quantities deep within Earth. It is the fifth most abundant element making up the planet, with most of it found in the outer layers of Earth's core. Volcanic activity brings sulfur to the surface, which is why it's found in large quantities around the brims of volcanoes and hot springs (possibly the reason for the name "brimstone").

Brimstone's link to hell was forged in fire. Sulfur burns easily and explosively, producing a gas that forms acid when combined with air and water. Ancient Egyptians burned sulfur in religious ceremonies 4,000 years ago, and it has long been used in China to make explosives and fireworks.

So when thinking about the fires of hell, sulfur—a flammable rock found in many places believed to be entrances to the underworld—seemed the perfect candidate as a fuel. And so, the fire and brimstone of hell were born.

Sulfur is bright yellow as a solid and odorless in its pure form. But combined with hydrogen, it takes on its nauseating rotten-egg smell. When burned, it produces an eerie blue flame and melts into a blood-red liquid. In other words, it's just about perfectly hellish.

It's also very useful. Sulfur is mined for use in many manufacturing processes, from oil refining and fertilizer production to preserving dried fruit. But traditional mining processes are notoriously dangerous, requiring people to work in volcanic areas surrounded by toxic fumes. Booker T. Washington once wrote, "I am not prepared just now to say to what extent I believe in a physical hell in the next world, but a sulfur mine in Sicily is about the nearest thing to hell that I expect to see in this life."

and open vents. But the features here are on a larger scale. There's the inky black Inferno Pool, with hot acidic waters that break down rock into mud, steaming cliffs where sulfurous vapors percolate through the rock, and boiling pools called Sodom and Gomorrah that sometimes erupt and gush water six feet (2 m) high. There's also Devil's Bath, a sulfur pool a Maori high priest once used for bathing, and another small pool once used to cook food, despite its black water and sulfurous smell.

The Hell's Gate area formed about 10,000 years ago when geologic activity drained a large lake. Without the weight of the lake's water, the land rose and cracked with the pressure of geothermal steam below. A series of eruptions then created the park's many features. Reportedly, its name came from the famous Irish playwright George Bernard Shaw who visited in the early 1900s and said the area "must be the gateway to hell."

If you catch yourself looking at one of Rotorua's hot mud pools and thinking, Gee, I'd like to jump in there—this is your chance. The most popular Hell's Gate attraction is a mud bath using sulfurous mud collected on-site. A worker totes buckets of the stuff each day from natural mud pools to geothermally heated baths, where you are given a 20-minute time limit (for safety reasons) to slather yourself with mud up to your nose, let it dry, then rinse off under showers.

Traditionally, Maori bathed in this mud to relieve joint and muscle pain and used the mineral waters to cleanse their wounds after battles. Today, warm mud baths are popular for relieving aches and pains and as a beauty treatment for the skin. Whatever their healing powers may be, mud baths definitely feel good. The fine clay mud envelops you like butter and then dries to a satisfying crispy shell. It's like being inside a croissant.

You will, however, smell faintly of sulfur afterward. But there's nothing like walking through a steamy hellscape and then getting up close and personal with it.

Wai-o-Tapu Scenic Reserve

A brightly colored volcanic landscape is a helluva spectacle.

Nestled among farms and forests on New Zealand's North Island is a landscape so vivid and colorful it defies all usual ideas of a hellscape. The park at Wai-o-Tapu bills itself as "one of the most surreal places on Earth," and it doesn't disappoint. This bucolic setting is the largest thermal area in the Taupo Volcanic Zone, the geologically active area that slices diagonally through the north-central part of New Zealand. This seven-square-mile (18 km²) thermal area is filled with steaming fissures and fumaroles, bubbling pools of mud, neon green acid lakes, and hot rainbow-hued pools.

In the Maori language, Wai-o-Tapu means "sacred waters." The lands here have been occupied and used by the Ngāti Tahu-Ngāti Whaoa people, a Maori iwi, for almost 800 years. The Maori have a principle called *kaitiakitanga,* meaning "guardianship," and they protect the land through traditional practices. They had a burial ground on the site and used many of the thermal pools, which range in temperature from tepid to scalding, for relaxation, healing, and for practical matters like cooking and cleaning.

Devil's Bath gets its neon hue from sulfur-containing minerals that reflect light in various shades of green and yellow, depending on the light.

In 1931, the government of New Zealand officially declared Wai-o-Tapu a scenic reserve, making it a protected area. Today it's called the Wai-o-Tapu Thermal Wonderland and is operated as a park by a local Maori tribal business.

Geological features in the park are labeled with their Maori names, as well as hellacious monikers invented by European settlers. Along the 1.8-mile (3 km) trail system, you'll stroll past a steaming crater called Devil's Home and oily black pools called the Devil's Ink Pots, in which acidic water is black from the ancient decayed remains of a swamp. The devil, it seems, has plenty to occupy his time at Wai-o-Tapu, and he's only just begun.

After you spend a couple hours wandering through a rainbow-colored hell, the landscape starts to become more drab at the end of the park's looping trail system. Then, just as you round yet another steaming fissure encrusted with sulfur crystals, there it is: A small scrub-covered hill plunges down into a volcanic crater filled with glowing green acid.

The Devil's Bath, or Roto Karikitea, is one of the park's most hellish features. The lake is a shocking hue of green-yellow that changes day by day depending on the sunlight and cloud cover. But whether you call it neon green, chartreuse, lime, electric—or radioactive—green, the water seems to glow from within.

The startling color comes from sulfur minerals suspended in the water refracting sunlight, which is why the color is at its most vibrant on clear sunny days. But even under cloudy skies, the effect is unnerving. The lake's water gets down to a pH of two, which is about the acidity of lemon juice. So falling into the Devil's Bath probably wouldn't kill you, or at least not right away, but it sure would sting.

As striking as it is, Devil's Bath certainly isn't the only hellish feature in the park. Just before reaching the neon green lake, you'll see Inferno Crater Lake, or Rua Pūmahu, a deep fissure in the rock with hot mud churning at its bottom. According to the park, the eerie sound of the bubbling mud pool was recorded and used as background in scenes of the grim land of Mordor in the *Lord of the Rings* trilogy, which were filmed in New Zealand.

The landscape here can be otherworldly in a more ethereal way, too. Some of the most colorful features in the park look like the pastel paintwork of the gods. The Champagne Pool is an orange-rimmed lake in a crater formed by a hydrothermal eruption 700 years ago. It gets its name from the bubbles of carbon dioxide gas that rise to the surface like champagne in a glass flute. Nearby, the Artist's Palette is a set of colored pools scattered across a large flat pan. Fed mostly by waters from the Champagne Pool, the palette breaks apart the rainbow into individual pools in a range of sky blues and sunset pinks, oranges, and yellows.

The "Hellhole of the Pacific"

The sleepy little island town of Russell off the North Island of New Zealand once held the title "hellhole of the Pacific." Today, the picturesque town boasts the oldest church in New Zealand, towering Norfolk pines (planted by missionaries), and a slew of charming beachside shops and restaurants. But according to local lore, it had a bawdy reputation in the 1800s as a port stop for sinful sailors. Russell reputedly had 70 grog shops and brothels, and hundreds of sailors from passing whaling ships would partake of their wares each day.

The variety of shades comes from the ratios of different trace elements in each pool—on brand, many are toxic—including sulfur (yellow) as well as arsenic and antimony (which combine with sulfur to create orange colors).

Most visitors start a day at the park at the Lady Knox Geyser, which erupts at 10:15 a.m. daily—with a little help. Park staff sprinkle a small bag of surfactant (essentially soap) into the geyser's gurgling mouth to create a foam that builds pressure in the geyser's chamber until it blows.

As the story goes, the geyser—and this nifty trick—were first discovered by a gang of prisoners. The prisoners of a low-security prison opened at Wai-o-Tapu in 1901 put soap in the water of the hot spring to wash their clothes, only to set off the geyser's eruption.

Now every morning, a crowd of people from around the world gathers to delight in this mega-version of a classroom science project. A minute or two after the soap is added, Lady Knox drools a bit of foam, and then with a great whoosh, a jet of water (surrounded by more than a few floating soap bubbles) shoots between 33 and 66 feet (10 and 20 m)

The multicolored Champagne Pool in Wai-o-Tapu Thermal Wonderland is as bubbly as its name implies, thanks to carbon dioxide gas seeping from below.

into the sky. The eruption lasts anywhere from a few minutes to an hour. Even though the geyser's labor is induced, it's still a great sight. No matter how international the crowd, everyone in the outdoor amphitheater reliably utters the universal language of wonder: "Ooooooh!"

🔱 BEFORE YOU GO

Wai-o-Tapu Thermal Wonderland is open Friday through Monday with the last admission at 3 p.m. and charges separate admission fees for the park and the geyser. If it rains, throw on some rain gear and go anyway. The park is still lovely, and you might see even more steam than usual. If you follow the park's recommended path, you'll end at the Devil's Bath. It also offers a café and small gift shop.

Waimangu Volcanic Valley

Earth's youngest volcanic hellscape was a forest 150 years ago.

On June 10, 1886, Mount Tarawera erupted. The blast was the biggest in New Zealand's recorded history, and it completely reshaped the landscape. Rocks and ash shot high into the air, pelting and then burying surrounding villages and wiping out life for miles around. A peaceful expanse of rolling forest became a craggy series of craters. Cracks and fissures opened up and allowed fluids heated deep in Earth to burst to the surface, creating bubbling, spitting mud pools and filling craters to form deep, steaming lakes.

As rescue parties rushed in, they were shocked to find what had been a lovely destination for Victorian-era tourists turned into a seething hell worthy of Dante's *Inferno*.

Even now, the land under hikers' feet is still slowly and subtly shifting, with new geothermal features constantly forming as fluids carve through the earth. Situated at the boundary of the Australian and Pacific tectonic plates in the Taupo Volcanic Zone, the park lies along the same "Ring of Fire" that creates earthquakes and volcanoes throughout the Pacific Rim. It runs just over two miles long (3.6 km) on easy walking gravel paths and boardwalks that end at Lake Rotomahana, a large lake composed of craters that filled with water in the years after the 1886 eruption. The lake was created by the blast, and below its surface lie some 200 hot springs.

Standing on a ridge looking across Waimangu Valley, with its lush trees and dotted jewel-toned lakes, it's hard to believe the entire landscape is less than 150 years old, but it is. Tarawera's eruption carved its lakes, fuming craters, steaming hot springs, and rare silica terraces. Welcome to the world's youngest geothermal environment.

With names like Inferno Crater and Frying Pan Lake, Waimangu's features are hellish in a strangely spectacular way. The scenic vistas at

Steaming cliffs fringe Lake Rotomahana, which formed after water filled in massive craters created by the eruption of Mount Tarawera in 1886.

A Hellish End to the "Eighth Wonder of the World"

In 1886, the largest volcanic eruption in New Zealand's recorded history rocked the North Island, destroying villages, killing more than 100 people, and fundamentally reshaping the region—including creating the stunning geothermal features now found in the Waimangu Valley. The eruption of Mount Tarawera also wiped out one of the world's geological treasures, the Pink and White Terraces, once known as the "eighth wonder of the world."

These enormous, terraced silica formations looked like mountains of molten candy and drew wealthy Victorian adventurers eager to see the bizarre landscape. Visitors would make a grand tour, traveling by boat from Auckland to Tauranga, then taking a horse-drawn coach to the shores of Lake Rotorua and on to the Maori village of Te Wairoa. After resting up at a hotel built to accommodate the growing tourist trade (stocked with the best wines and liquors to be found in the bush), hotel staff in the morning would pack a picnic lunch and Maori guides would take their guests by boat and then on foot for a day of frolicking in the hot pools puddled on the terrace ledges.

But in the early morning hours of June 10, 1886, tragedy struck. At that time, the volcano was composed of three distinct peaks visible to the northeast of the terraces, and in the weeks before the eruption, it gave hints of misbehaving.

Surveyor Henry Roche witnessed the eruption and described "a wall of fire 1,500 feet high." When the sun rose that morning, it revealed a devastated landscape. A great rift 11 miles long (more than 15 km) had split the earth open in a gash running from the volcano to the southwest, creating what is now the Waimangu Volcanic Valley. This newly created canyon became the simmering landscape we see today. The small Lake Rotoma-hana with the Pink and White Terraces on its shores was replaced by an enormous crater and a new Lake Rotomahana, 20 times the size of the original.

Underneath the massive lake lies what remains of the eighth wonder of the world. The delicate, sparkling silica was smashed to bits by the eruption before it disappeared under the water. In 2011, researchers found fragments of the Pink and White Terraces deep below the lake's surface.

Today, visitors to Waimangu Volcanic Valley can take a boat tour of Lake Rotomahana and pass over the spots where the terraces once towered. Swans float gracefully along a peaceful shore, and boats pass steaming fumaroles and burbling hot springs along the rocky cliffs that form the crater's edge. If you're lucky, you may see a geyser erupt just at the edge of the bay. All around, the cliffs still have some of the pink and white colors that made the terraces so spectacular.

As the boat captain reminds his passengers, we've lost the sights that once were, but we've gained the new and amazing landscape that's here now. And if there's one constant in this dynamic place, it's change. This valley is a chance to see Earth's forces not only in action but also in fast-forward mode.

Waimangu also can't be matched. For those who prefer their hell on the pleasant side, and not smelling too much of sulfur, Waimangu is sure to delight.

A hike through the valley, which is protected as a scenic reserve, begins with a shaded passage though the green subtropical forest that has regrown since the eruption. The first crater lake you'll come upon is the aptly named Emerald Pool. Because the small lake is at the southern end of the park, farthest from the volcano, its waters are cool enough to support flourishing mats of algae and sphagnum moss, which give it its dark green color.

You won't have to walk far before you crest a hill overlooking the Emerald Pool's near opposite: Frying Pan Lake. Picnic tables at a lookout spot offer a fantastic view of one of the world's largest hot springs—and also one of the deadliest. This steaming lake occupies Echo Crater and earns its scalding name with waters reaching 131°F (55°C), hot enough to cause third-degree burns in 30 seconds. Dangerous as it is, the steam rising from the deep-blue lake is mesmerizing. At first, it looks as if the lake is permanently shrouded in fog, then you realize that the "fog" is rising from a spot above the geyser near the lake's center. From there, it swirls toward the shores in a never-ending show that shifts with the breeze.

Nearby lies Inferno Crater Lake in a crater blown in the side of Mount Haszard in the 1886 eruption. The crater shares a mysterious underground connection with Frying Pan Lake: Water flows between the two lakes in complicated rhythmic cycles that vary in length, with one lake overflowing as the other recedes.

Here, you'll see eerily pale crystal blue waters made partly opaque by high concentrations of silica, topped by a head of swirling steam. White silica deposits frame the lake's edge. Though it looks almost like a giant heated swimming pool, you wouldn't want to take a dip. The water temperature can reach 176°F (80°C), and the acidic pH can be as low as 2.2.

Continue on, and the geothermal features become more spread out, but also more hellish-looking. You'll see a near-boiling stream and steaming cliffs and fumaroles. Then a pleasant hike through mostly native bush gives the chance to spot a few endemic New Zealand birds and plants before culminating on the shores of Lake Rotomahana.

Though the stunning silica terraces are no more, the lake's shores are still geologically active. You'll get the best views of the enormous crater high on Mount Tarawera, where the mountaintop blew on that day in 1886, and everything changed for this little corner of the world.

♆ BEFORE YOU GO

Book ahead of time for a boat ride around Lake Rotomahana, where you'll see the sites of the former Pink and White Terraces. Afterward, stop at the nearby Te Wairoa village, where you can see excavated and rebuilt remains of the village that the volcanic eruption buried in 1886.

Red aquatic fern contributes to the gory hue of the water in the Southern Crater's lake in Waimangu Volcanic Valley.

Yellowstone National Park

The devil would be right at home in one of America's favorite national parks.

Yellowstone may already be on your bucket list of vacation destinations, but it turns out, a visit there will also count as a trip to hell. Situated mostly in northwestern Wyoming and spilling into Montana and Idaho, Yellowstone National Park straddles a hot spot created by one of the world's largest known active volcanoes, the Yellowstone Caldera, resulting in a geothermal wonderland filled with exploding geysers, burbling mud pots, and rainbow-colored hot springs.

In fact, the park's lands have been compared to hell since the early 1800s. John Colter, a member of the Lewis and Clark expedition, reported wandering through a strange world where the earth was warm and smelled of rotten eggs, and steaming hot water erupted from the ground. After his experience in 1807 and 1808, people jokingly called the area "Colter's Hell." Decades later, the area was more thoroughly mapped and was found to be just as incredible as Colter had described it. And in 1872, Yellowstone became the United States' first national park.

The park boasts more than 10,000 thermal features, including hot springs, geysers, mud pots, travertine terraces, and fumaroles (see the Geology of Hell, page 27). Yellowstone is home to at least half the geysers on Earth—more than 500 of them—which are formed when a constriction in the plumbing of a hot spring causes pressure to build until water erupts. One of the best places to find Yellowstone's hellish hydrothermal features is in Norris Geyser Basin, the oldest and hottest of the park's thermal areas, where boardwalks wind past rare acidic geysers and vibrantly colored hot springs.

Do not, however, make the fatal mistake of leaving the boardwalk. Underneath the thin, hollow crusts nearby lies scalding hot, acidic water. A dip into one of Yellowstone's hot springs, which can reach temperatures up to 198°F (92°C), can be fatal within minutes. At least 22 people have died after falling or jumping in, according to park historian Lee Whittlesey's book *Death in Yellowstone: Accidents and Foolhardiness in the First National Park*.

The park's geyser basin areas, home to hot springs and geysers including Old Faithful and Grand Prismatic Spring, are another must-see. Grand Prismatic, often called the rainbow hot spring, is the largest hot spring in the United States and is spectacular to look at, but also dangerously hot and toxic. The blue water at its center could give you a third-degree burn in under a second. Cyanobacteria called *Synechococcus* produce the yellow pigments in the next hottest band, followed by a more diverse mix of life in the cooler outer rings.

The park has plenty more hellishly fantastic sights. Make sure to include these on your tour, too:

The Terraces at Mammoth Hot Springs: These huge travertine terraces are formed by hot springs that underlie limestone deposits. Calcium carbonate dissolves and is deposited as calcite that builds up over time. These large white terraces are still growing and shifting, and they offer a rare chance to see large terraces like those of the lost eighth wonder of the world, the Pink and White Terraces of New Zealand (see page 189).

Grand Prismatic Spring is often called the "rainbow" hot spring for its cheerful colors, but don't be fooled—its waters are scalding hot and toxic.

Anemone Geyser: This geyser doesn't shoot high into the air, meaning you can get close to it and be entertained by watching it fill up every few minutes, erupt with a splash, then drain like a toilet being flushed.

Morning Glory: The vibrant deep blue of this hot pool in Upper Geyser Basin was nearly lost after years of people throwing trash, coins, and rocks into the pool. The situation got so bad that by the 1950s, the pool was nicknamed "Garbage Can." Since then, efforts to protect the pool and clean out the trash have partially restored it, but new microbes that grow around its edges have given it more of a rainbow-hued effect.

Wyoming: Hell State?

Wyoming calls itself the "Cowboy State," but it could also lay claim to a darker designation. At least 22 places in the state have the word "devil" in their name, plus at least five use the name "hell," according to the news outlet *Cowboy State Daily*.

The most famous of these sites may be Devils Tower (and nearby Hell's Hole) in northeast Wyoming, where a massive butte rises high above the prairie. Like other huge geological features, the tower seems tailor-made to inspire visions of either hell or an alien world. As such, it made the perfect site for the climax of the movie *Close Encounters of the Third Kind,* in which a group of UFOs drops off their cargo of alien abductees at the tower.

Yellowstone National Park has a hot spring cone called Devil's Thumb and a dangerous gas-spewing cavern called the Devil's Kitchen in the Mammoth Hot Springs area, plus a valley called the Devil's Den and a fishing spot at Hellroaring Creek. Elsewhere in the state are mountain peaks called Devil's Graveyard and Devil's Tooth, and ravines and passes with names like Devil's Gap and Devil's Gate. There's also the vast, spiky canyon known as Hell's Half Acre, used for filming *Starship Troopers,* another alien-invasion movie.

So as you embark on a tour of the Cowboy State, keep your eyes peeled for devilish place-names. They tell us something about the mindset of the settlers who named them in the 1800s, when the Wild West must have looked like a landscape devised by the devil himself.

ETHIOPIA

Danakil Depression and Erta Ale

A scorching desert, smoking mountain, and ancient fossils combine in the "Hellhole of Creation."

Where three tectonic plates meet in the Horn of Africa, a special place has emerged. As the plates slowly pulled apart over millions of years, they left at their junction a sunken spot in Earth's crust, known as the Afar Depression. Its northern end is home to one of the most inhospitable deserts on the planet, the Danakil Depression, and one of Earth's few active volcanoes that holds a fiery lake of lava. Yet, within the Afar Depression, scientists have found the oldest fossil remains of our human ancestors, making this region potentially the cradle of humankind.

The volcano here is called Erta Ale, which means "smoking mountain" in the local tongue. Not only is the volcano home to one of the world's few persistent lava lakes (see page 141), but it also often hosts two, in separate craters. Because of its lava lakes and location in an ancient cradle of humanity, Erta Ale has been called the Hellhole of Creation.

The Danakil Depression is the hottest place on Earth in terms of average year-round temperatures. It's also one of the lowest places on the planet at 330 feet (100 m) below sea level, so like Death Valley, it's shielded from weather and gets almost no rain. Combine all that with the ongoing geologic activity beneath its surface, and this is an unrelenting hell.

But it's also one of Earth's most stunning landscapes, making it a surprisingly popular destination for travelers seeking out the planet's most unique and extreme environments. The salty desert is painted in brilliant yellows, oranges, and neon green from minerals brought to the surface by volcanic activity. There are acid pools, mountains of salt, steaming fumaroles, and shooting geysers in sulfurous hot springs. It's a wonderland of geology to rival that of New Zealand's volcanic region, but in a far more desolate and remote setting.

Among the features to see in the Danakil Depression is the Gaet'ale Pond, one of the saltiest natural bodies of water on Earth. At 43 percent salinity (mostly calcium chloride and magnesium chloride), it handily beats out the Dead Sea (34 percent). Because it's also heated by volcanic activity, the pond's water can reach a temperature of more than 150°F (65°C)—hot enough to immediately scald, not that you'd want to swim there. Odorless gases also bubble up through the pond, and dead birds are sometimes found around it. Most likely, carbon dioxide produced by volcanic activity is responsible for suffocating the wildlife, so be careful in approaching it.

George Kourounis, an explorer who has gotten up close and personal with some of the planet's most dangerous places, said of Erta Ale that "if there's any place that's a gateway to hell, this has got to be it." Kourounis joined a scientific expedition to the volcano in 2005 when Erta Ale was one of the most inaccessible places in the world, in addition to being one of the hottest. (Since then, roads and development have made the volcano more accessible.) He wanted to rappel into the crater and get as close to the lava as he could. When he finally reached the summit, after a 17-hour camel trek in blazing heat, he found that the volcano's activity had ramped up, and lava now overflowed the ledge he had planned to rappel down. Kourounis was lowered 60 feet (18 m) into the smoking crater of the volcano and walked—gingerly—on the crust formed by cooled lava. Smoking black chimneys called hornitos rose around him, their tips glowing, and it was as close to the feeling of walking through hell as Kourounis says he's ever had.

Though most travelers won't want to get quite that close, it is possible to see some of the region's most stunning features more safely. In recent years, adventure guides have made it easier to get to the area, offering tours that go to the rim of Erta Ale to witness the boiling lava and to the area around Dallol, a mining town that is now sparsely populated but has long held the record of the hottest inhabited place on Earth.

The bizarre and beautiful landscape around Dallol, an abandoned mining site, has made the ghost town a popular, if unusual, tourism destination.

PART THREE

OTHERWORLDLY
DESTINATIONS

t's time to explore those places on Earth that are so strange, so beyond the ordinary, that they can only be described as otherworldly. Each of these destinations has some hellish feature, but unlike our previous chapter, they're not quite literal hells on Earth. Instead, our otherworldly locations take on aspects of hell—such as death, monstrous creatures, or perilous landscapes—that are as varied as the underworlds of cultures around the world.

After all, not all hells are full of fire and devils. One of the most famous hells, Hades, was believed to be a bleak and gloomy landscape but still full of fields, forests, and rivers. Then there's the decidedly more pleasant ancient Irish otherworld Tír na nÓg, an enchanting land of supernatural beings where it's always springtime and youth lasts forever.

Likewise, the otherworldly places we set out for in this chapter are more eerie than fiery. These are places that feel as if they came

Glowworms suspend their bioluminescent bodies over the water on long sticky threads, hence their Maori name *titiwai,* or "projected over water."

PAGE 200: Ol Doinyo Lengai, known as the "Mountain of God" to the Maasai people, is the only volcano known to spew thin, silvery lava, which is said to flow too fast to outrun.

out of a dark, sometimes twisted, fairy tale. Think *once upon a time, there was a strange land where...* a strange land where thunderstorms never end. A strange land where glowing creatures hang like stars in the sky. A strange land where the forest is made of knives. And all of these are real strange lands, right here on Earth.

Any one of them could be someone's vision of the underworld. When I think of the underworld, I can't help picturing the Upside Down from the Netflix series *Stranger Things*. In this ghostly realm, monsters roam a landscape that looks like a dark, burned-out version of the world we know. It's an "otherworld" dimension adjacent to ours that occasionally pulls someone in. You might also imagine the weird landscapes of Oz or Narnia, or even the world of another celestial body, such as Idaho's Craters of the Moon (page 226).

Some landscapes aren't described in any culture's lore about hell, but seem like they should have been. Here, I'm thinking of places like the Naica Cave of the Crystals in Mexico (page 206), where sparkling selenite crystals the size of tree trunks sprout from the walls of a steaming hot cave. Or the Tsingy de Bemaraha in Madagascar (page 218), where a thicket of razor-sharp rocks rises from the ground. And in Indonesia, the volcano Kawah Ijen (page 247) stands apart for the brilliant blue flames that roll down its crater walls.

Then there are the extreme destinations. We'll go to Lake Maracaibo in Venezuela (page 244), the most lightning-prone place on the planet, where a seemingly never-ending thunderstorm hovers over one spot. Also Peru's Boiling River (page 240), where the hottest of hot springs creates an entire river that simmers like a witch's cauldron.

Other destinations in this section are more eerie than dangerous. Two places have formations that look like giant skulls: Australia's Skull Rock (page 234), an island surrounded by shipwrecks, and northern England's Hodge Close Quarry (page 237), which has gained fame for the skull that appears reflected in its ice-cold water. By way of death-themed destinations, we'll take a look at the Fengdu Ghost City in China (page 250), a place where you can pregame the afterlife by walking all the steps the dead take on the path to reincarnation.

Creatures are also often associated with the underworld, from the serpents of Brazil's Snake Island (page 267) to the giant bats of Kasanka National Park in Zambia (page 254) to the creepy-crawly ecosystem of Malaysia's Gomantong Caves (page 211). And for the greatest concentrations of real-life monsters on Earth, we'll head to Cape York, Australia (page 263), where the wildlife includes aggressive crocodiles, deadly vipers, and venomous sea creatures.

So, did someone leave the gates of hell open? It might seem so when you start exploring places where a bit of the underworld seems to be leaking into reality. Rest assured, all the strange phenomena you're about to encounter have perfectly rational scientific explanations. But throughout history, many have seen more mysterious forces at work.

Cave of the Crystals

A deadly cave holds a passage to a magical, shimmering realm.

Mexico's Cave of the Crystals is often compared to Superman's famous Fortress of Solitude. It could also be described as what hell might look like if the devil got really into crystals.

Workers exploring a newly drained portion of a lead and silver mine in Naica, Mexico, discovered the cave in 2000. The mining company pumped water out of the cave, hoping to find more metals, but what was found instead turned out to be one of the world's most spectacular natural wonders, with enormous milky white crystal pillars spilling every which way inside a massive cavern. The largest among them are more than 30 feet long (10 m) and are estimated to weigh 55 tons (50 t). But very few people have witnessed this sparkling spectacle: It's also a death trap.

Because it's located nearly 1,000 feet (300 m) underground, you might expect the cave to be pleasantly cool year-round. In photographs, the crystals look like huge blocks of ice, adding to the illusion of a frozen wonderland belowground. But the reality is anything but chill. Thanks to a pool of piping hot magma lurking beneath the cave, air temperatures inside reach more than 120°F (50°C) with humidity levels around 99 percent, which can feel like an intolerable 228°F (108°C).

"It feels like you're getting hit in the face with a sledgehammer when you first step in," says George Kourounis, an explorer and storm chaser who has sought out many of the planet's most extreme environments. It took him two years of planning to visit the cave for one day. He had a film crew with him to record the epic adventure—and an ambulance on standby in case something went wrong.

Your body can't shed heat in that environment, making the cave's conditions potentially fatal within 15 minutes. In fact, one miner who tried sneaking into the cave to steal crystals lost consciousness before he

A miner's shrine sits among selenite crystals taken from the Cave of the Crystals.

could get back out and was later found dead. So to safely explore the cave, Kourounis had to don a special cooling suit with chilling packs and a backpack respirator that allowed him to breathe cooled air. Even with the suit, he could only be inside the cave for a maximum of 45 minutes.

There, Kourounis found himself clambering among crystals the size of giant tree trunks. The crystals are made of selenite, a crystallized form of the mineral gypsum used in drywall. The cave's crystals grow so large because of the cave's unusual environment. Before the cave had been drained, mineral-rich 136°F (58°C) waters filled it for more than half a million years, allowing the crystals to slowly form underwater.

The world's biggest crystals are found in the flooded caves of the Naica Mine. They formed over millions of years in mineral-rich waters.

That steamy environment is decidedly hellish, Kourounis says. "Oppressive is an understatement," he says. "Every cell in your body is telling you to leave. Except your eyes—your eyes want to drink in every moment of it because it is so overwhelmingly beautiful."

The rest of us may never have the chance to see this terrible beauty. The cave was discovered only because the mining company in Naica had pumped the scalding hot water out of it. Scientists were able to explore the cave using cooled suits, albeit briefly, even finding weird microbial life trapped inside the crystals. Explorers also found adjacent caves, including a large network of caverns, beneath Naica. But after mining operations ceased in 2015, the site, including most of the caverns, was allowed to once again flood with groundwater.

So for now, the Naica cave is the one hellish place in this book that's truly inaccessible. But on the upside, as Kourounis says, while the cave is flooded, the crystals are able to continue growing, undisturbed. That means this sparkling wonder is at least well preserved for the time being.

Gomantong Caves

Squeamish beware: This cave is filled with roaches, bats, and spitting birds.

f your idea of hell involves many-legged creepy-crawlies, this cave in Malaysia might qualify. For the rest of us, it's an eerie but exciting look at the many kinds of life that skitter, flap, and squirm underground.

The Gomantong cave system is found in Sabah, Malaysia, on the island of Borneo. Its two main chambers, the Black Cave and the White Cave, are famously home to approximately two million wrinkle-lipped free-tailed bats, along with enormous, stinky piles of their feces, called guano. Add on top of that a healthy layer of roaches and centipedes that live off the guano, and the critters that in turn eat those insects, and you get the picture. It's an entire ecosystem built on bat poop.

The large limestone caverns, with ceilings up to 300 feet high (90 m), are also renowned for thousands of cave swiftlets that build their nests there. These insect-eating birds have their own creepy quirks: Not only can swiftlets echolocate like bats, but they also build their nests entirely out of their own saliva. Glands under the birds' tongues secrete a gummy substance—it's white, yellow, or a dark brown-red, depending on the birds' diet—that the birds spit into sticky threads and then weave into hammock-shaped nests. Once the threads harden, the translucent nests look like a spider's web that has frozen solid.

The Gomantong Caves offer gorgeous underground views for those who can look past the roaches, spiders, and centipedes that live here in multitudes.

The nests are harvested twice a year to make bird's nest soup, a controversial delicacy of Chinese cuisine. No one knows who first decided to soak and eat a swiftlet nest, but for generations bird's nest soup has been sought as an elixir for youth and vitality. The process of gathering nests for the soup involves collectors climbing up precarious rattan ladders and bamboo poles to pluck the nests off rock walls high above the cave floor. (To protect the swiftlet population, nests are collected only before the swiftlets lay eggs—spurring the birds to build a second nest for laying—or after fledglings have left the nest.) The used nests have to be rinsed clean of feathers and bird poop before being used in the soup.

The Black Cave is the more accessible of the two main caverns and is open to the public. Inside, visitors will find millions of cockroaches climbing the walls and floors—some tourists describe them crunching underfoot—plus plenty of spiders, rats, and snakes. The cave gets its name from black-nest swiftlets and the dark-colored nests they build. The White Cave, meanwhile, contains the closely related white-nest swiftlets, which make pale-colored nests. The White Cave requires a caving permit and appropriate equipment to visit, plus a steep 30-minute climb to reach the entrance. During nest harvests, you might even get to see collectors at work gathering the more highly prized white nests.

The surrounding forest is also a protected area rich in wildlife, from the bat hawks that pick off bats emerging at night to langurs, macaques, and orangutans. A popular option for spotting wildlife is to take a cruise on the Kinabatangan River through the tropical lowland rainforest, with a stop at Gomantong Caves.

⚕ BEFORE YOU GO

As of summer 2023, the park had suspended entry inside the caves, citing maintenance and repair, but the rest of the park is open, up to the cave entrance. Please check with the Sabah Wildlife Department or tour operators to make sure the cave is accessible before going, or plan to stay outside and watch at dusk as millions of bats emerge from the cave, and the swiftlets fly in to take their place overnight.

The black nests are traditionally harvested in April and August, and the white nests are harvested in February and August.

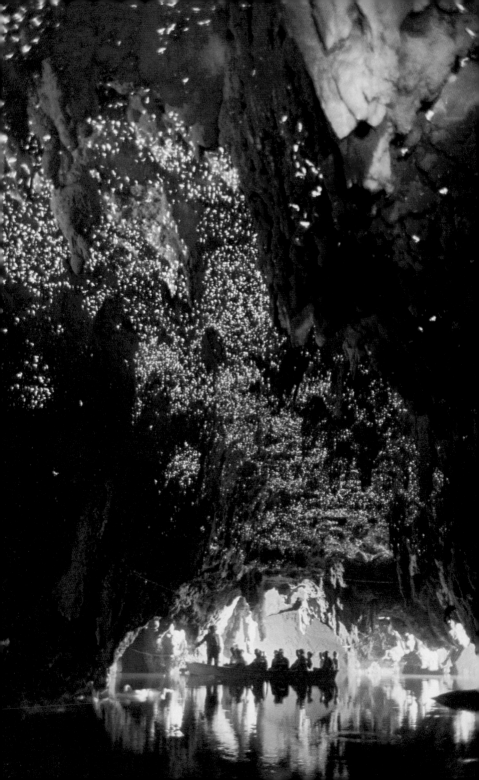

Waitomo Glowworm Caves

Float through a magical wonderland of glowing maggots.

n the cool darkness of Waitomo Glowworm Caves, 15 hushed visitors and I shuffle single file into a small flat-bottomed boat and take our seats. Quietly, so as not to disturb the glowworms, we sail into the blackness. Soon, specks of bluish green light begin to appear overhead, and then deeper into the cave, a constellation. Like magic, thousands of tiny glowing lights sparkle overhead and are reflected in the stream below.

The starlike lights are made by New Zealand glowworms (*Arachnocampa luminosa*, a species name that would make a great Harry Potter spell). At the larval stage, the cave-dwelling insects look like small worms and produce light through bioluminescence, hence glowworms. The guides will tell you, however, that the luminous glowworms attracting visitors from all over the world to these New Zealand's caves aren't actually worms—they're maggots, larvae of flies called fungus gnats. "But I

The blue-green lights of glowing fly larvae, also known as maggots, have become one of New Zealand's most popular attractions.

(

don't think we'd get many visitors if it was called 'glow-maggots cave,'"
jokes a guide. Like many of the guides here, he's a descendant of the Maori
family that has long owned and operated the Waitomo Glowworm Caves.

And though the lights are beautiful, they're also deadly. The preda-
tory glowworms use their lights as lures, attracting hapless fliers into
their sticky traps, then reeling them in to be eaten alive. The glowworms
can only catch prey this way by living in the dark, still environment of
a cave. When you look at it that way, this otherworldly sight seems a bit
gruesome.

In the Maori language, the glowworms' name is *titiwai,* meaning
"projected over water." That name makes sense when you see the silk
threads hanging from the cave ceiling—up to 30 per insect, each thread
dotted with sticky droplets secreted by the glowworms. They use the
droplets to capture prey, including other glowworms. That's right, these
are cannibalistic maggots, too.

Maggots or not, the tiny insect larvae are stunning in large numbers. They're endemic to New Zealand and are found in many caves on
both the North and South Islands. The larvae are born on the cave walls
and grow to more than an inch long (30 to 40 mm) over several months,
then become flying adults that look a bit like mosquitoes and live only
another few days—during which their only goal is to reproduce.

The Waitomo Glowworm Caves were first explored by Maori chief
Tāne Tinorau in 1887. He, along with English surveyor Frederick Mace,
entered the caves on a flax-stem raft with only candles for light. They
were amazed to float past huge numbers of the glowing creatures as they
navigated a stream running through the cave's passages and soon began
bringing visitors in to share the wondrous sight.

In 1904, New Zealand's Department of Tourist and Health Resorts
took over the caves. In 1990, a protracted legal battle resulted in the
return of the caves and surrounding lands to their original Maori owners,

who now run the cave's tourism operation in association with the Department of Conservation. Many of the descendants of these owners (including great-great-grandchildren of Tāne Tinorau) still work at the caves.

Today, visitors can tour up to three caves at the sprawling site, which is located about a three-hour drive from Auckland. The Waitomo Glowworm Caves tour includes both the boat ride and a walk through the limestone cave, with its large chambers, stalactites and stalagmites, and other cave formations that have been millions of years in the making. A walking tour of Ruakuri Cave includes a more close-up view of the tiny creatures. And Aranui Cave is a large dry cave (with no stream or glowworms) that offers the most magnificent cave formations and a chance to see the native cave wetas, giant long-legged crickets with humped backs.

🔱 BEFORE YOU GO

The three Waitomo caves are spread across a large area. So, if you're going to multiple caves, make sure to visit them in the order you've booked. There's also another magical boat journey through a glowworm cave at Spellbound, less than a 20-minute drive away and managed separately.

The Waitomo area isn't the only place in New Zealand to see glowworms, though it is the most established. If you're staying in Rotorua, you can arrange a nighttime walking tour to a glowworm cave. Glowworms also live in caves and gorges in Whangārei, Waiomio, and Tauranga on the North Island, and Te Anau and Hokitika on the South Island, among other places.

Tsingy de Bemaraha

A bizarre rock formation creates a devilishly sharp landscape.

xplorer George Kourounis calls it "the devil's obstacle course," a dense forest of razor-sharp rocks, able to tear through flesh like a knife. And you don't have to wait for the afterlife to experience the thrill of suspending yourself over a deep chasm filled with giant pointy spikes that could easily impale you.

Madagascar's Tsingy de Bemaraha National Park and adjacent Tsingy de Bemaraha Strict Nature Reserve are located in western Madagascar, a large island off Africa's east coast. The word *tsingy* (pronounced "sing-ee") comes from a Malagasy word meaning "where one cannot walk barefoot," a clear reference to the huge block of Jurassic limestone that water has eroded to form deep crevices between tall spires. Over millions of years, layers of harder rock have been exposed and honed to razorlike spines, some as tall as skyscrapers, others waist-high.

This is the world's largest tsingy forest, with nearly 600 square miles (1,550 km²) of pinnacles that can reach up to 2,600 feet tall (800 m). It's divided into areas known as the Great Tsingy and the smaller Little Tsingy.

"It's this diabolical mix of limestone spires and spears, and every single plant is encrusted in thorns," says Kourounis, who explored the wildest part of the Tsingy in 2014, looking for caves and dinosaur tracks. "This entire region has no other purpose than wanting to rip you to shreds."

If this isn't sounding like an appealing destination yet, you should know that visiting this forest of needles in Madagascar is not only a chance to explore a landscape like no other, but also to see plants and animals found nowhere else on Earth. Lemurs such as the white Von der Decken's sifaka leap among the tops of the needles, oblivious to their pointy peaks. Parrots and bats roost in the mid-levels, while tiny mouse lemurs and dwarf chameleons populate the floor.

Sifaka lemurs climb the sharp stone pillars in the Grand Tsingy to scout for a meal.

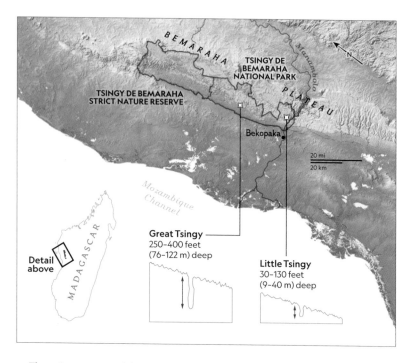

The spiny canyons of the Tsingy de Bemaraha formed largely belowground as deep, narrow caves. Monsoon rains chiseled into the limestone from above, while groundwater dissolved the stone from below. Eventually, cave roofs collapsed and what was left behind was a labyrinth of steep canyons called grikes.

Most of the species that live in Madagascar are endemic, and many of those are endangered. For some of them, the tsingy is a perfect refuge, so impenetrable that hunters, hungry cattle, and other large predators avoid it. So this rough terrain has become a perfect place for spotting rare wildlife—as long as you don't mind navigating a labyrinth of pointy rocks.

You can explore parts of the tsingy from the ground, winding your way through sharp rocks, or try out the aerial suspension bridges in the national park to see the rocks from above. On the Ranotsara Trail, you'll cross a 60-foot (18 m) bridge made of rope and wood hovering

230 feet (70 m) above the spiky ground. The experience will send shivers down your spine, even if you're clipped to the bridge with carabiners. Though people use the bridges every day, they have been featured on lists of the world's scariest bridges. In the southern part of the park, which includes the higher-peaked Grand Tsingy and the Petit Tsingy (or Little Tsingy), several hiking and climbing routes with ladders and bridges will take you all the way up the Great Tsingy for spectacular views—you'll be harnessed and safely tethered with climbing equipment along the way, but you'll still get the excitement of swaying to and fro over deadly serrated rocks.

BEFORE YOU GO

Tsingy de Bemaraha National Park is open in Madagascar's dry season, from April to November, but the Great Tsingy is open only from June to November. The reserve area is undeveloped for tourism and requires a permit for entry.

Guides and climbing equipment are available at the national park headquarters in the village of Bekopaka.

Deception Island

An icy landscape conceals a secret passage into an active volcano.

A voyage to Deception Island has the fantastical elements of an epic journey into the underworld. In the middle of an alien landscape shaped by rock and ice, you can find yourself floating in the sea, and at the same time inside the heart of an active volcano.

You see, nothing about Deception Island is quite what it seems. From a distance, it appears to be a normal, solid island. But once you sail through the narrow passage into its interior, you find yourself inside a ring with massive rock walls rising from all sides.

The island is actually the very tip of a volcano rising above the ocean. The Deception volcano erupted violently about 4,000 years ago, causing its summit to collapse and form a caldera more than four miles wide (7 km). The caldera filled with seawater and formed the "lake" in the island's interior. But that doesn't mean the volcano has been tamed: In fact, it has erupted multiple times since seal hunters first documented it in 1820.

To get inside, you must pass through a tight channel called Neptune's Bellows, named for the dangerously strong gusts of wind that howl through the passage, as if the Roman sea god Neptune were blowing a trumpet. Once past that obstacle, you're still not safe. Explorers and hunters have tried to use Deception as a base of operations since it was discovered, none successful in the long term. First, massive over-hunting pushed fur seals to near extinction in the South Shetlands within a few years of the island's discovery. (Their populations rebounded after hunting stopped, but scientists fear that climate change is pushing them back into decline.) Then in the early 20th century, Norwegians built a whaling station there, complete with a radio station, whale-processing station, and a cemetery. All these failures led

Those who venture into the interior of Deception Island are met by chinstrap penguins on its steaming shores, warmed by the volcano below.

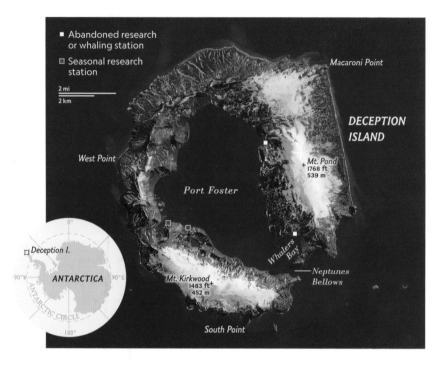

The explosion of an Antarctic volcano around 4,000 years ago ejected so much magma that the volcano's top collapsed and formed a caldera, now filled with water as the interior of ring-shaped Deception Island.

to the notion that the island, or at least those who try to exploit it, may be cursed.

Research bases also sprang up nearby but were abandoned in 1967 when the volcano erupted and forced evacuations. In 1970, the Deception volcano erupted again, causing massive mudflows that buried buildings and closed the whaling station for good.

Despite the island's desolate location and extreme environment, it's home to a thriving community of wildlife that's worth the risk of a visit. One of the world's largest colonies of chinstrap penguins nests there, and the volcanic ash allows lichens and moss to survive.

Today, thousands of tourists visit Deception Island each year. Many simply get a view of the island from a distance, because large cruise ships cannot approach too closely for fear of hitting obstacles near the island, such as Raven's Rock, a hazard lying just eight feet (2.4 m) below the surface.

But those on smaller ships that do pass through Neptune's Bellows and into the island's inner cove are treated to stunning views of black sand beaches, crater lakes, and towering cliffs. For the few people who have managed to disembark onto Deception Island itself, there's no mistaking its volcanic nature. The waters along the shore steam thanks to hydrothermal heating. Some tourists even don bathing suits and frolic in the warm waters on Deception Island, with icy mountains as a backdrop. Just dig a hole and let it fill with volcanically warmed water from below, and you've got yourself an Antarctic hot tub.

Craters of the Moon

A volcanic landscape takes you into another world.

n 1969, four lunar astronauts stepped onto an eerie, cratered landscape like nothing they'd ever seen on Earth. But these astronauts weren't on the moon. They were in eastern Idaho, preparing to go to the moon on the Apollo 14 mission. That meant going to a place on Earth with an alien surface: Idaho's Craters of the Moon.

In fact, even though it's located just a few hours' drive from Yellowstone National Park (see page 193), Craters of the Moon is so otherworldly that it has become a favorite place for scientists to study what other planets might be like. In 1969, the astronauts needed to learn to recognize volcanic features similar to those on the moon's surface, and Craters fit the bill.

Today's visitors to the national monument are treated to an eerily beautiful volcanic sea set amid fissures, lava fields, lava tubes, craters, and cinder cones. The pockmarked landscape is often described as lunar. Some people feel like they're hovering light-years above Earth, while others feel like they've fallen into an underworld inside Earth's core.

Lava flows over the past 15,000 years have created the weird landscape of Craters of the Moon. Today, more than 53,000 acres (21,500 ha)

This otherworldly passageway is an enormous lava tube called Indian Tunnel, a cavern formed by a river of lava.

Lava flows at Craters of the Moon create a landscape so alien that NASA scientists have studied its features as an analogue to Mars.

of volcanic landscape and lava flows fill the 750,000-acre (303,514 ha) park. The environment ranges from sagebrush steppe teeming with wildlife such as sage grouse, pronghorns, and mule deer to stark lava fields where rivers of dark lava are frozen in time. A 52-mile-long (84 km) crack in Earth's crust, called the Great Rift, also runs through the geologic wonderland. All in all, what you end up with looks like it could be the blackened, desolate landscape of hell in a Hieronymus Bosch painting.

One of its most unusual features might also be its most hellish. Craters of the Moon has an abundance of lava tubes, natural caverns formed by the flow of lava from a volcanic eruption. When the top of a lava flow cools enough to harden and insulate the molten rock inside, it forms a tube, and once all the lava has run out of the tube, what's left behind is a pipe-shaped tunnel through the earth.

Today, visitors to Craters of the Moon can duck inside lava tubes (open during the summer) to experience the wonder of a journey into the earth for themselves. Inside one of these tubes, you'll feel like you've entered a passage to the underworld. The floors and walls are ropy and uneven; drips of lava that have cooled and hardened remind you that molten lava once rushed through the channels you're standing in now. One of the biggest, Indian Tunnel, has 30-foot-high (9 m) ceilings and extends 800 feet (244 m) into the earth, making it seem like an enormous borehole to hell.

In 2017, *National Geographic* documented the work of NASA scientists who mapped the Indian Tunnel lava tube using laser scanners called lidar (light detection and ranging) to create a detailed three-dimensional view. The researchers hope to use what they learn from Earth's lava tubes to prepare for human exploration of Mars, which also has a network of lava tubes beneath its surface. Early visitors might need to hide out from Mars's intense radiation and extreme weather by sheltering inside these subterranean labyrinths.

Once you've surfaced from the underworld, top off your day by heading to the Lava Flow Campground. There, you can spend the night surrounded by lava rocks. It's a little like camping out in hell, once it's cooled off a bit.

♆ BEFORE YOU GO

To enter the lava tube caves, you'll need a permit from the park—but getting one is easy. Just ask for one at the visitors center. They'll do a quick screening to make sure you aren't carrying a fungus into caves that is harmful to bats.

Lake Natron

A blood-colored lake is home to the heavenly sight of pink flamingos.

Tanzania's Lake Natron is a salty red lagoon that stands out from its dry surroundings like a drop of blood on the landscape. But despite its spooky appearance, the lake is home to one of the world's most spectacular sights: more than two million flamingos gathered in fluffy pink drifts along its shores.

For most animals, the lake is as unfriendly as it looks. It gets its name from the naturally occurring mixture of sodium carbonate compounds in the lake called natron, which ancient Egyptians used to mummify the dead because it's so good at drying out things. Evaporation has concentrated these minerals over time, making the water so salty and alkaline that little can survive in it. As if that weren't unpleasant enough, the lake is fed by hot springs that can push it to 120°F (49°C). Not many plants or animals can tolerate such harsh, toxic conditions, but a small number of species have adapted to—and actually flourish in—this uninviting water.

The lake is a crucial breeding ground for lesser pink flamingos, which get their color from eating the salt-loving microorganisms, including cyanobacteria and archaea, that give the lake its red and orange colors, too. In fact, the lesser flamingo pretty much relies on the lake for its continued existence, with an estimated 75 percent of the birds born at the lake. The flamingos' tough, leathery legs help them withstand the stinging salt water, which has such high mineral content that it's described as feeling viscous to the touch.

When water levels in the lake are just right, lesser flamingos fly in from other saline lakes in the region to build their tall conical nests in the water. The water has to be high enough to create a toxic moat that keeps predators from snatching up the flamingos' eggs, but low enough not to flood the nests. Only then does a mama flamingo lay a single egg, which both parents incubate. The little gray chicks hatch between

Lake Natron gets its fiery red color from microorganisms that can tolerate its hot, salty waters.

December and February, meaning that even in hell you can catch the sight of thousands of cute little fuzzy babies.

Some fish also manage to live in Lake Natron, at least part-time. When the lake level is low, a few species of tilapia are able to survive in stream-fed lagoons around the lake's edge. There, hot springs provide the minerals that feed algae, which feed the fish and the flamingos.

Visitors can expect to see flamingos nesting between August and October, and can try to spot other animals in the area too, such as zebras, wildebeests, gazelles, and ostriches. The lake is also near Ol Doinyo Lengai, an active volcano that occasionally erupts with lava rich in carbonatite. The thin, silvery lava is said to flow from the volcano faster than a person can outrun it.

It's a strange and forbidding place in many ways, but a must-see for its surreal beauty.

Skull Rock

A forbidding death's head rises from the sea.

From Wilsons Promontory, the southernmost point on Australia's mainland, an eerie sight can be seen on the horizon. Off in the distance, what looks like an enormous, craggy skull rises from the ocean.

This is Cleft Island, often called Skull Rock. From certain angles, this oblong chunk of granite appears to have empty holes for eyes peeking above the waves, much like a skull lolling to the side. From other vantage points, it looks like a bird's skull, and the closer you get, the more skull shapes you'll see within it. Making the whole experience even more foreboding, the seafloor around Skull Rock is studded with shipwrecks, as if the rock is warning sailors of danger for all who dare enter here.

The skull's largest gaping "eye socket" is actually a 430-foot-wide (130 m) cavern, big enough to hold the Sydney Opera House. Its entrance is carpeted in green grass and filled with cormorants and Cape Barren geese, a lovely oasis that just begs to be entered and explored. But vertical cliffs and treacherous waves make it nearly impossible. As a result, few have been inside the deep cavern; locals say that only nine people have ever pulled off the feat.

The best way into the cave requires abseiling (rappelling) down ropes from a helicopter, a James Bond move that isn't going to be on

Large caves that look like eye sockets give Skull Rock its forbidding name.

most tourists' to-do list. But in 2015, a team led by archaeologist and television presenter Neil Oliver did just that. They reported finding old cannonballs, presumably from passing ships taking potshots at the creepy rock.

But there is another way to get a look at Skull Rock up close. Rugged powerboats now offer tours that get closer than ever before, offering views of the diverse wildlife that lives on and around it. Thousands of fur seals hang out on the rocks and islands in the surrounding Bass Strait, and many seabirds nest there, including sea eagles, little penguins, shearwaters, fairy prions, and Pacific gulls.

♆ BEFORE YOU GO

Cleft Island sits in the Wilsons Promontory Marine National Park about three miles (5 km) south of Tidal River, the main visitors center for the park. Cruises to view the island depart from Port Welshpool or Port Albert. Pennicott Wilderness Journeys operates amphibious boats that take you onto Norman Beach as well as around the island; those cruises depart from Tidal River.

Hodge Close Quarry

A creepy illusion makes this cavern look like an entrance to hell.

t's been called Britain's scariest cave. When reflected in an ice-cold lake in the north of England, a cavern and rocks at the bottom of a deep quarry create the ghostly image of a skull. The spooky spot is popular among hikers, divers, and thrill seekers who abseil (rappel) down the quarry walls, but beware—the lake's cold, 100-foot-deep (30 m) water has claimed several lives.

Hodge Close Quarry is a massive excavation of slate near Coniston, Cumbria, in northwestern England, not far from Scotland's border. The place looks like the set of an Indiana Jones movie, with massive boulders strewn about and towering 150-foot-tall (45 m) gray-green stone walls draped in moss. You can view the quarry from a parking area above, but to truly see the skull effect, you'll want to scramble down a small, rocky path to the water's edge (the trail begins about half a mile [0.8 km] from the parking lot, hidden well enough among the trees to make it feel like a secret).

Poked into one wall of the quarry are two holes leading into one large cavern. From inside the cavern, it feels like you're looking out through the "eyes" of a skull. But from the outside, catch just the right angle and the hole on the left mostly disappears, while the one on the right remains a dark void. Tilt your head 90 degrees to the left, and the skull illusion appears, with the void reflected in the lake to form the skull's eyes. A nearby pile of fallen rock forms the skull's gaping jaws.

It's such a creepy visual effect that Hodge Close was used as a filming location for the Netflix series *The Witcher* in the episode "What Is Lost" as the place where dead Witchers, monster hunters with supernatural abilities, are laid to their final rest. Now, adventurers and fans of the show come to see the skull effect and take in the cavern's soaring ceiling in person.

The creepy reflection of a skull in the lake at Hodge Close Quarry guards an underwater cave that has claimed several lives.

The lake has also become a go-to location for technical divers looking for a challenge. The network of underwater caverns is considered extremely dangerous and has claimed a number of lives. Others have died diving from the cliffs above or from shock in the freezing waters (less than 50°F/10°C). Only experienced divers with special cold-water equipment and dry suits should consider attempting to enter the caverns.

⚱ BEFORE YOU GO

Hodge Close Quarry is about a 15-minute drive down narrow country roads from the village of Coniston. From the small parking area, enter the rocky path down to the lake at the south end of the quarry. Divers often enter the quarry lake by following a creek through an old mining tunnel to a rocky ledge above the lake. Note: Diving is not regulated here, so go at your own risk. The large cavern forming the skull's eye can be entered from behind via another rocky path through the woods.

Boiling River

**If a river through hell could be beautiful,
it might look like this.**

There are times when the Boiling River is invisible, hidden beneath a fluffy cloud. Other times, the fog lifts and the river reveals itself: turquoise waters burbling over pale, smooth stones. It looks inviting, but don't hop in. This river lives up to its name, reaching temperatures up to 207°F (97°C), hot enough to cook you like the devil's stew meat.

The thick shroud of vapor is not the only way the Boiling River hides itself. Tucked in a dense jungle with no roads nearby, the river went virtually unnoticed by outsiders for centuries. Its existence was a closely guarded secret among the local Asháninka people and shamans who regard the hot waters as sacred. It was the furthest thing from a tourism destination.

So when geoscientist and National Geographic Explorer Andrés Ruzo first started recounting stories about a mysterious boiling river that he had heard of from Peruvian relatives, his colleagues thought he was nuts. Sure, one told him, boiling rivers are a thing, but only near volcanoes. There's no volcano within hundreds of miles from where the Boiling River was thought to be.

But Ruzo was determined to find out if the river was real. His aunt had been to the river decades earlier, and the pair decided in 2011 to go

National Geographic Explorer Andrés Ruzo takes a bridge across Peru's mysterious "boiling river," which was a local secret until he trekked there in 2011.

find it again. At that time, it took a two-hour drive from the nearest city, Pucallpa, followed by a motorboat ride and long hike to reach the river. (Today, it's just a three-hour direct drive from Pucallpa to get there.)

The journey was well worth it. "There was something magical about the place that was just, I mean, the word 'enchanting' is the only thing that can come to mind," Ruzo told host Peter Gwin on National Geographic's *Overheard* podcast. Even though the water is hellishly hot, the setting is ethereal—even heavenly.

The steaming turquoise waters run for about four miles (6 km) and reach 16 feet (5 m) deep and 80 feet (24 m) wide in places. As Ruzo has discovered, the mysterious source of the river's heat is a geothermal

242 | GO TO HELL

fault; water flows into the fault and is heated by Earth's interior, then shoots back up through cracks to the surface. Because the water is hottest near the hot springs that feed the river, it's possible to walk downriver and find waters tepid enough to take a dip.

Ever since his journey to the river in 2011, Ruzo has been on a mission to save it. And that, he says, means that you should come see it. He's been working with two traditional healing centers on the river to help them expand their ecotourism operations while preserving the surrounding jungle, which, like most of the Amazon, is threatened by deforestation and resource extraction. "Our goal is responsible development that empowers and benefits those who live in the area," he says.

A Boiling Lake in Dominica

Like a witch's cauldron, the Boiling Lake in Dominica's Morne Trois Pitons National Park bubbles and churns under a roiling cloud of steam. It's a fantastic sight, tucked high in the jungle where only the adventurous get to see it.

The lake is actually a flooded fumarole, with a volcanic vent spewing a mix of hot water, steam, and gases into its basin. And it is literally boiling; even the water along the edges of the lake is too hot to touch, so don't even think about a swim. At more than 200 feet (60 m) across, this is the second largest hot lake in the world, after Frying Pan Lake in New Zealand (see page 188).

Getting to the lake, which lies at an altitude of 2,600 feet (790 m), requires an eight-mile hike (13 km) with a climb up the mountain Morne Nicholls, then through the aptly named Valley of Desolation. Tour operators offer guided hikes.

Learn about the local plants and their medicinal qualities at the Mayantuyacu healing center. Then, after hiking to the river and looking for wildlife, enjoy a soak in the cooler section downriver. Before nightfall, look for *la hora del vapor* ("the vapor hour"). At this time, the cooling air generates large plumes of steam on the river, and it's one of the best times to unwind and enjoy the dreamy landscape.

🔱 BEFORE YOU GO

The Boiling River is known locally as Shanay-Timpishka and is at the center of the small town of Mayantuyacu. Here, you'll find two shamanic centers, Mayantuyacu and Santuario Huishtin, and lodging at Shanay Timpishka Ecolodge.

Lake Maracaibo

The world's lightning capital gives a taste of the weather of the damned.

High in the night sky, bolts of blue, pink, and white lightning pierce through glowing storm clouds. Below, coconut trees sway between houses rising on stilts from a dark lagoon. Welcome to the lightning capital of the world.

The light show here, where the Catatumbo River flows into Lake Maracaibo, is so famous that it has its own name: Catatumbo lightning. This electrifying show of nature's power happens up to 300 nights a year, peaking in September. It can be seen for miles around, creating a kind of natural lighthouse that has also given it the name the "Beacon of Maracaibo."

Some call witnessing the Catatumbo lightning a mystical experience; others might describe it as a hellish and never-ending storm. But no one who comes to this lake near the Andes Mountains in northwest Venezuela walks away unimpressed.

The region has the highest concentration of lightning on the planet (more than 200 flashes per square kilometer each year) and includes the point with the most lightning strikes on Earth: 1.2 million zaps a year.

Throughout most of the year, a giant thunderstorm forms every night over a vast area of almost 2,000 square miles (5,100 km²). Though it may seem the devil is at play, there's a perfectly good scientific explanation for the nightly show: At sunset, cool air rolls off the mountains and runs into warm, moist air rising from the lake. Colliding particles of rain and ice crystals high in the air create a negative charge that builds up in the clouds until it's released as a massive discharge of electricity—that is, lightning bolts. Most lightning moves from cloud to cloud, but

Enormous thunderstorms gather over Lake Maracaibo almost
every night of the year, making this the most electric place on Earth.

some strikes the ground, channeling up to a billion volts of electricity into whatever is unlucky enough to be in its path.

Lake Maracaibo gets so much lightning because of its special geography. The Andes and two other mountain ranges enclose the lake on three sides, creating the perfect conditions for the atmospheric convection that drives thunderstorms. Plus, Lake Maracaibo, which is actually a brackish bay that opens to the Caribbean Sea, is South America's largest body of water. That means plenty of steamy air fuels thunderstorms.

Visitors can fill their days watching the area's abundant wildlife, including monkeys, exotic birds, and freshwater dolphins. Then it's time to rest up, because the lightning show is at its most spectacular after midnight. Such a rare and special place deserves a spot on the bucket list; look forward to one day taking in Venezuela's lush rainforest, tropical beaches, and rocking electrical light show.

BEFORE YOU GO

The Catatumbo lightning peaks in September and is at its least frequent during the dry season of December through February. Most overnight tours originate out of Mérida, a university town surrounded by the Andes Mountains, and include an overnight stay in a *palafito* (stilted house) where you can safely watch the lighting from under roof cover.

Tourism to Venezuela has been strongly curtailed in recent years by an economic crisis and civil unrest, making travel there more difficult, so check the current status before you plan a trip.

Kawah Ijen Volcano

A diabolical mountain erupts in blue flames and sulfurous fumes.

Ghostly blue flames roll down the sides of the volcano known as Kawah Ijen, glowing and roiling like a neon wraith. If it weren't so beautiful, it would be terrifying. Not every traveler, after all, is willing to don a gas mask and climb into the crater of a volcano spewing sulfurous gases—that are *on fire,* no less—but the willing few get to experience one of the world's most beautiful hells on Earth.

It looks as if blue lava is cascading down the sides of the crater—and sometimes down the entire mountainside—but there's actually no lava involved. Instead, the eerie blue effect arises from burning sulfuric gases emitted by the volcano that ignite and burn blue when exposed to oxygen in the air. Some of the gas condenses to a liquid, and this burning liquid sulfur creates the illusion of flowing blue lava.

Kawah Ijen is part of the large Ijen volcanic complex on the eastern side of the island of Java. Although it's in a remote area, guided tours bring visitors to the mountain from cities on Java and from the neighboring island of Bali. Most visits begin at night, because although the blue flames of Kawah Ijen burn 24 hours a day, they're invisible until night falls, when they stand out against the darkness. The most reliable place to see the fire, though, is inside the volcano's crater itself; there, brilliant flames shoot from cracks where sulfuric gases are escaping.

Flowing sulfur ignites to create the ghostly blue flames that flow on Kawah Ijen.

A typical tour arrives at Ijen around midnight to hike to the crater through a rainforest filled with giant ferns. Wearing a gas mask, you'll hike into the crater to see blue fire before returning to the rim for a sunrise view above the stunning turquoise acid lake that sits in the base of the crater.

The lake looks like a gorgeous swimming hole, but like everything else about Ijen, it's not to be underestimated. The beautiful aquamarine color comes from a mix of caustic hydrochloric and sulfuric acids, and taking a dip would mean almost certain death—of the slow and painful variety, where your flesh is dissolved off the bone.

When National Geographic Explorer George Kourounis went to Ijen, he paddled a rubber raft out onto the acid lake in one of the mountain's craters—a terrifying proposition considering that he first stuck an aluminum soda can in the lake, which immediately started to fizz and sizzle. But in he went, the raft made it through, and he was able to measure the lake's pH: about 0.5, more acidic than battery acid.

Mining the mountain for its sulfur, which is used to process sugar on Java, is one of the world's most dangerous and difficult jobs. Heavy chunks of solid yellow sulfur are chiseled out with crowbars, loaded into baskets, and carried by hand on a 2.4-mile (4 km) trek up and out of the crater, then down to the base of the mountain.

The miners often go without the gas masks given to tourists, wearing only wet cloths wrapped around their faces to dampen the fumes. The acid they breathe in burns the miners' lungs and inflames their throats, and carrying loads heavier than 150 pounds (70 kg) at a time can deform their spines and bend their legs. Today, tour operators often encourage visitors to donate their gas masks to miners at the end of their trip.

The combination of the ethereal but deadly acid lake, toxic gases, and dazzling blue flames makes Kawah Ijen a special and truly hellish place—the reigning king of blue flame.

Fengdu Ghost City

This ancient city dedicated to the afterlife still haunts today.

The Fengdu Ghost City isn't your usual ghost town. Yes, there was once a city called Fengdu here on Ming Mountain. Yet this isn't just a city that's been abandoned, but rather a sacred place said to be haunted by ghosts from the underworld.

The city of Fengdu is believed to be at least 2,000 years old and is filled with structures, statues, and artwork related to Diyu and Naraka, the hells of Chinese mythology and Buddhism. The city's sprawling complex of temples, shrines, and monasteries originally served as a burial site and place of worship. But it also took on a dark reputation. According to Chinese legend, two Taoists named Yin Changsheng and Wang Fangping came to Ming Mountain to worship and become immortals. Combining their names produces "Yinwang," meaning "the king of hell." And so, Fengdu became known as the place where the king of hell (called Yama in Buddhist teachings) lives.

The Three Gorges Dam project, which was finished in 2012, flooded much of the original city of Fengdu, which was rebuilt higher up the mountainside with the same name. Today, what's left of the old city serves as an instructional guide to death, with monuments depicting the tests that await souls before they can be reincarnated, as well as the

Fengdu is known as the "Ghost City" because of its legendary connection to the Chinese afterlife. Sculptures depict souls being tortured in hell.

tortures that sinners must endure in death. It's a mix of old buildings and new and now serves as a popular tourist attraction highlighting traditional beliefs about the afterlife.

Located on Ming Mountain near the Yangtze River, the Ghost City has become a popular stop for boat tours, along with the Three Gorges Dam. The construction of the dam, with the world's largest hydroelectric plant, not only flooded the Ghost City but also cut it off from the rest of the province. Fengdu can now only be accessed by stairs or a chairlift from the river's edge.

Once there, visitors take a trip through Chinese visions of the underworld, which arise from a mix of Buddhism, Taoism, and Confucianism. This purgatory, called Diyu or the "earth prison," is believed to exist inside a giant mountain—some say it's the very mountain on which Fengdu was built—and is often described as a maze with various levels where souls atone for the sins they committed while alive.

First, though, the dead must pass various tests and tribulations. And at Fengdu Ghost City, you can test yourself in real-world versions of these trials. You begin by crossing the Bridge of Helplessness (or Bridge of Troubled Water), where souls are judged. There are different protocols for crossing the bridge depending on your sex, age, and marital status; today, a popular "test" is to cross the bridge in as few steps as possible for good fortune.

Next, the soul must be judged by Yama, king of the underworld, who metes out punishments depending on the sins committed during life; these are carried out in the various levels of hell and must be completed before the atoned soul can move on. (See more in 18 Levels of Hell, page 175.) In today's Ghost City, this is represented by a garden filled with large statues of demons and dioramas depicting the punishments of hell.

Finally, the ruler of the last court of hell, Zhuanlun Wang (or Chuan-Lun-Wang) spins the dead on the Wheel of Rebirth to determine the reincarnated soul's fate the next time around. People today approximate this final test by standing on one foot for three minutes at the entrance to Tianzi Palace in Ghost City.

According to legend, once the dead have completed this entire process, they get to enter the "Last Glance at Home" tower to see and say goodbye to earthly life. They drink a special soup made by a woman called Old Lady Meng, or Meng Po, goddess of forgetfulness, that erases all memory of past lives, and then they can be reincarnated.

So, to complete your journey to Fengdu's Ghost City today, you can take in views from a tower built in 1985 to symbolize the Last Glance at Home. While you're there, you can imagine the next, and maybe better, life that may be yet to come.

Kasanka National Park

Millions of giant bats make for a spine-tingling safari.

Zambia's Kasanka National Park is home to one of the world's greatest, and spookiest, spectacles. Each year, millions of giant bats come here from across Africa to gather in a small patch of swamp forest. It's Africa's—some say the planet's—largest mammal migration, and it fills the skies over Kasanka with a dark cloud of rustling wings every evening as the bats take off en masse—yes, like bats out of hell.

An estimated 10 million or more straw-colored fruit bats congregate in what's aptly called the Bat Forest of Kasanka, a type of swampy evergreen forest known as *mushitu*. The bats are the second largest fruit bats on the continent, with a wingspan up to three feet (1 m). They come here to stuff themselves on seasonal fruit, pollinating flowers as they eat and making themselves invaluable to the tropical ecosystem.

And because they're not hiding out in caves like most bats, you can get a much closer look at the bats of Kasanka while they roost. Straw-colored fruit bats are named for the golden collars around their throats, which contrast with their dark leathery wings. With their long, narrow faces and golden yellow eyes, it's easy to understand why bats have long been likened to demons and underworldly creatures.

From the visitor platforms, you'll get a great view of the bats over the tree canopy. The bats roost in such massive numbers there that they literally weigh down tree branches to the point of breaking. Even though the bats are nocturnal, they're fun to watch during the day. A bat coming in to roost will climb over its sleeping compadres to find a

Millions of straw-colored fruit bats return to their daytime roosts in Kasanka's swamp forest just before sunrise.

The World's Biggest Bats

The straw-colored fruit bats of Kasanka National Park are megabats, a fitting name for the biggest bats on Earth. The megabats make up the family *Pteropodidae* and are also known as fruit bats or flying foxes, named for their foxlike faces.

The largest megabat is the giant golden-crowned flying fox, which has a wingspan up to 5.5 feet wide (1.7 m). The biggest-bodied is the great flying fox, which tips the scales at up to 3.5 pounds (1.6 kg). If that doesn't seem all that big, imagine a Yorkshire terrier with a two-foot (0.6 m) wingspan flying at your face.

spot, then drop upside down to groom, pee, poop, and catch some shut-eye.

Daytime is also a good time to spot the animals that eat the bats. When a branch overloaded with bats falls, scavengers rush in to clean up the injured and dead. This is when you'll spot servals, crocodiles, pythons, vultures, and even leopards moving in for a bat snack. Several species of eagles, falcons, and kites will also swoop in to pick off a bat when they can.

In the evening, you can see the spectacle of millions of bats rising from the trees and filling the air as they leave for their nightly feast. At dawn, come back to see their return, which some say is even more breathtaking, as the bats' silhouettes stand out against the reds and golds of the sky at sunrise.

Kasanka is one of the country's smaller parks, at 160 square miles (420 km²), but also one of the most diverse, with forests, lagoons, rivers, lakes, and wetlands. Kasanka is a great place to see bushbuck (a type of antelope) along the forest edge, Kinda baboons, and blue monkeys. Birders will be especially rewarded, with 479 documented species in the park—from wattled cranes and the rare Pel's fishing owl to Böhm's bee-eaters and trumpeter hornbills.

🔱 BEFORE YOU GO

The straw-colored fruit bats converge in Kasanka Bat Forest in October and typically stay through the end of December.

Bracken Cave

Witness the world's biggest emergence of bats out of hell.

As the sun sets over a summer-baked Texas Hill Country, bats begin to emerge. For a few moments, they trickle out from a 100-foot-wide (30 m) hole in the earth, but then the entire colony of millions of Mexican free-tailed bats seems to rush for the exit all at once, gushing from the cave in a wave that crescendos upward into a swirling mass of brown wings. It looks like an army emerging from the underworld.

Since up to 20 million bats can try to get out of the cave during any given evening, it takes a while, usually two to three hours. As the bats emerge, they circle around to fly north en masse, and in their circling create what's aptly called a "batnado." This tornado of bats rises high into the air then splits off into streamers that flow like giant, winding ribbons through the sky.

Bracken Cave Preserve, east of San Antonio, hosts this spectacle every night during the hot Texas summer. It's home to the largest bat colony in the world, which is quite possibly the largest single gathering of mammals anywhere on Earth. It's also a maternity colony, populated entirely by female bats that fly (while pregnant) about 1,000 miles (1,600 km) north from Mexico in March and April to give birth to a single pup, which they raise in Bracken Cave until it can fly and hunt insects on its own.

Bracken Cave is home to the world's largest bat colony, creating a nightly spectacle as female bats and their young pups emerge by the millions.

The cave itself is a shallow 650-foot-long (198 m) cavern with a sinkhole as its entrance, creating what looks like a wide-open mouth at the bottom of a low rise. Inside, guides say, the cave is about 175 feet high (53 m)—as measured from the floor of guano, or bat poop, to the ceiling. The guano pile itself is estimated to be more than 70 feet deep (20 m), and its ammonia smell wafts from the cave entrance, fanned by millions of bat wings.

When you visit, you'll be watching the bats emerge from an open viewing area that is plenty close enough to take in the aroma and to see some bats flying directly overhead. Luckily, the sight of the batnado will distract you from the smell; more difficult is remembering to keep

Like a Bat Out of Hell

Bats have long been associated with demons and hell, perhaps unsurprisingly because they're known for flying out of caves and tend to do so as night falls. Adding to their devilish charm are those leathery wings, sharp little teeth, and eerie ability to navigate in complete darkness.

One of the first written references to bats and the underworld was in Homer's *Odyssey*, written around the eighth century B.C. There, ghosts, or "shades," in the underworld are described as flitting about and gibbering like bats in a cave. And in the Old Testament books of Leviticus and Deuteronomy, bats are listed among the animals considered unclean.

But the idea of bats as creatures of hell really came into its own with the rise of Christianity. The early Christian writer Tertullian described demons as having wings, and Basil of Caesarea posited in the fourth century A.D. that whereas angels fly on feathered wings, demons soar through the air using fleshy wings like those of a bat. From there, imaginations took off. Dante's version of Satan in *Inferno* had three faces, with two enormous wings below them described as larger than the sails on a ship and covered not in feathers but in skin like a bat's. And in Duccio's painting "Temptation of Christ on the Mountain," the devil himself not only has batlike wings but also hooked heels like those bats use to cling upside down to cave ceilings.

Even today, bats can't shake their dark reputation. They're staples of Halloween decor—a holiday itself derived from the ancient Irish festival of Samhain (see page 53). And thanks to Irish writer Bram Stoker's inspiration of blood-drinking vampire bats, the nocturnal creatures will be forever imagined as the doppelgängers of vampires like Dracula. Even comic-book hero Batman keeps the bat light on, with a storyline featuring Barbatos, a batlike villain based on a demon from the ancient book of demonology *Ars Goetia*.

your mouth closed as you gape up in awe—you don't want to catch the kind of raindrops that fall from a bat cloud. Once you've taken in the batnado for a while, walk the short trail to the other side of the sinkhole and learn more about the bats from docents on hand with cave rock samples and other displays, and see a mine shaft where Bracken Cave's guano was once mined to manufacture black gunpowder during the Civil War.

The bats amaze both young and old alike (my 10-year-old great-niece rightly pronounced the sight "mesmerizing"). Equally fascinating is the story of what's happening behind the scenes in the bat cave, which you can't enter for both the bats' safety and your own (don't forget about that seven-story pile of guano). Deep in the cave, the female bats have set up crèches, or nurseries, where newborns can keep each other warm while the moms are out making a living, eating their own body weight in insects each night. This means a mother bat must find her own baby among the millions of others, packed in at up to 400 pups per square foot, every time she needs to feed it. She accomplishes this through an incredible combination of spatial memory, plus recognizing her own young's vocalizations and scent.

The babies are born in June, and by late July they're testing out their wings. Bat moms and youngsters fly from the cave and can ascend to heights up to 10,000 feet (3,050 m), flying as high as many airplanes. There, they hunt for insects, including huge clouds of moths migrating high from field to field.

If you're an early riser, you can opt to watch the return of the satiated bats to Bracken Cave in the morning, with flights starting around 5:30 a.m. The bats approach the entrance from above, requiring each bat to perform a last-minute flip to enter the cave's narrow mouth, and this flip produces a "ch" sound that multiplies by the millions of jostling bats to create a buzzing, whooshing sound like no other.

Whether you visit in the wee hours or in the evening, it's an awe-inspiring sight, and just about guaranteed to make you fall in love with these furry, flying hellions.

🔱 BEFORE YOU GO

The nonprofit group Bat Conservation International owns and manages the land that Bracken Cave sits on, and to protect the bat colony, viewings are allowed only with reservations made in advance. Visit the group's website to see when tickets for the next bat season will be made available, usually in March. Mark your calendar because spots go quickly. The site has a viewing area with benches but limited amenities.

Cape York

**Deadly creatures await in
Australia's wildest territory.**

No book about hell would be complete without a few monsters. And one of the best places to see the most fiendish beasts outside the underworld is Cape York, a peninsula jutting toward Papua New Guinea from the northeastern shore of Australia.

Cape York encompasses the largest pristine wilderness in Australia, with scenic savanna, rainforest, and wetlands edged by more than 1,000 miles (1,600 km) of coastline. It's considered one of the most beautiful and unspoiled parts of the country, a fisherman's paradise, and a popular destination for Australians seeking off-road adventures. But within these wilds are some of the most frightening creatures found on the earthly plane: enormous saltwater crocodiles, deadly snakes, and an assortment of venomous spiders and stinging insects.

The waters are no less treacherous. You could find yourself floating next to one of the most venomous animals in the world: the box jellyfish. The sting from this blob of goo can kill you in under five minutes. Or you might be dodging deadly species of fish, octopuses, and sea snakes. In fact, just don't go in the ocean at all, because there are also man-eating tiger and bull sharks in there. And while you're at it, be cautious about the beach—pick up a pretty seashell containing a cone

snail and the creature inside might shoot out a little harpoon of poison powerful enough to kill you.

Of course, many Australians will tell you this is paranoid talk—the spiders aren't even all *that* poisonous, and there are just a handful of fatalities from all these animals each year. Most visitors will make it through an entire trip to Cape York without so much as seeing a saltwater crocodile, as long as they're smart enough to stay away from places where the reptiles congregate, like river mouths. And despite all its dangerous creatures, the cape is a great place to spot some of Australia's most beautiful and unique wildlife, such as platypuses and echidnas, bandicoots and quolls (carnivorous mammals), cassowaries, parrots, and blue-winged kookaburras, not to mention marine mammals like dugongs, whales, and dolphins.

But then, the saltwater crocodiles are no joke. An awful lot of local news stories about goings-on in Cape York seem to involve "salties," as they're known. There's a story about a salty attacking campers in a tent on the beach. Then there's the man who barely fended off an attacking crocodile by stabbing it in the eye. Worse, two crocodiles were shot and cut open to look for the remains of a missing fisherman. (Unfortunately, they found him.)

So, if you want to see saltwater crocs while you're in Australia, Cape York probably isn't the safest place to go looking for them. You'd do better to take a cruise in Kakadu National Park, or visit other parks in the Northern Territory or Western Australia with regulated viewing areas. Australia's saltwater crocodiles can grow to be up to 20 feet long (6 m) and weigh more than a ton. They'll eat just about anything, including sharks, and have no fear whatsoever of humans. On average, several croc attacks

Cape York is home to many of Australia's most dangerous animals, including saltwater crocodiles that are notorious for attacking humans.

happen each year in Australia and one or two of them are fatal, all on the north coast and all by saltwater crocs. Freshwater crocodiles ("freshies," of course) are also common there, but they rarely bite unless provoked.

Also cropping up in the Cape York area are reports of increasing encounters with the common death adder, which despite its horrific name isn't Australia's most dangerous snake. That title belongs to the eastern brown snake, ranked second most poisonous land snake on Earth and responsible for many of Australia's snake-related fatalities (which average a few a year).

Overall, you're very unlikely to be killed by any of Australia's dangerous creatures—but tourists who get attacked by wild animals have often put themselves in harm's way, either by approaching animals (no crocodile selfies, please!) or ignoring good advice like putting away food at campsites.

So if you go, check out what naturalist Steve Backshall, host of the BBC program *Deadly 60,* called "the home of deadly" and prepare to stay safe. The most adventurous travelers often set out for Cape York itself, at the tip of the Cape York Peninsula. This is the northernmost tip of Australia, and it's also quite inaccessible with limited roads and services. If you're not experienced with off-road vehicles, consider a guided tour where the driving and logistics are handled for you—plus your guide can help you spot wildlife safely.

Even if you're careful, you're just about guaranteed to see a few deadly monsters in Cape York. Just make sure to give them the proper measure of respect—after all, you're in their hell now.

⚟ BEFORE YOU GO

Many travelers begin a trip across the peninsula in the city of Cairns and make their way north. You can head up via four-wheel-drive on the historic Old Telegraph Track, the original path of telegraph lines through Cape York, crossing creeks and stopping to swim in the magical (and croc-free) Fruit Bat Falls. Or take a coastal route and stop for wildlife watching and waterfalls in the parks along the way.

Snake Island, Brazil

Serpents have long been linked to hell and the devil, from the Garden of Eden to descriptions in Dante's *Inferno*. This island named for its slithery inhabitants and home to some of the deadliest snakes in the world may just be hell on Earth.

Ilha da Queimada Grande, also known as Snake Island, is located about 90 miles (145 km) off the coast of São Paulo, Brazil's largest city. Most residents there have heard tales about people who ventured onto the island and were killed by snakes—including, supposedly, the last lighthouse keeper to live on the island in the 1920s before it became completely unpopulated. Though rumors claim pirates brought the snakes there to protect buried treasure, scientists say the snake population got there naturally and boomed after rising sea levels cut off the island from the mainland 11,000 years ago.

Now several thousand golden lancehead vipers, one of the deadliest snakes in the world, dominate the island. The snakes on the island evolved with more potent toxins than mainland vipers, all the better to allow them to quickly kill migratory birds, their main prey. That toxin is so powerful that a single bite can kill a human in an hour's time.

In fact, it's so dangerous that tourism is no longer allowed on the island. Visits are strictly controlled by the Brazilian Navy and are limited to scientific research and navy personnel.

The lava lake atop Mount Nyiragongo in the Democratic Republic of the Congo offers a view into a roiling hellscape.

Destinations by Location

Acknowledgments

I still have to pinch myself to believe it's real: National Geographic not only allowed me, but actually encouraged me, to write a book about hell. It's been such a pleasure, and the adventure of a lifetime, to travel to many of these places and research the ones I haven't been to—yet.

I would like to thank the amazing creative team at National Geographic Books for their enthusiasm and unflagging devotion to this book. Special thanks go to my editors Allyson Johnson, whose sharp editing kept me on track ("But what makes it *hellish*?"), and Tyler Daswick, who made sure my voice came through on every page. Thanks also to the entire Books team, including Heather McElwain for excellent copyediting, Jenny Miyasaki for proofreading, photo editor Susan Blair for the amazing photography, and designer Nicole Roberts for making this slice of hell so gorgeous. Thank you also to creative director Elisa Gibson, director of photography Adrian Coakley, and production editor Becca Saltzman, for all your work making this book come to life.

I couldn't have written *Go to Hell* without the support of my friends, family, and colleagues. Thank you to all those who contributed ideas for hellish places or endured long conversations about hell,

274 | GO TO HELL

including my nephew, writer John Austin Baltisberger, John Travis, Christina Callicott, and the Traditions crew, including Sue Calcote, Lydia Pulsipher, Laura Moll, and Steve Blackwell.

I'm especially grateful to those experts who have been generous with their time and knowledge about these places. A special thank you to archaeologist Daniel Curley of the Rathcroghan Visitor Centre, explorer George Kourounis, Prior La Flynn of Lough Derg, and my guide to the Phlegraean Fields, Paolo Mondola.

Finally, to my faithful travel companions Mindi Gondek, Kate Travis, and my husband, Jay Gulledge, thank you for going to hell with me.

Selected Bibliography

Alvarado, Denise. *Witch Queens, Voodoo Spirits, and Hoodoo Saints: A Guide to Magical New Orleans*. Weiser Books, 2022.

Bailey, Lloyd R. "Enigmatic Bible Passages: Gehenna: The Topography of Hell." *The Biblical Archaeologist* 49, no. 3 (September 1, 1986): 187–91.

Brady, James E., and Holley Moyes. "The Heart of Creation, the Heart of Darkness—Sacred Caves in Mesoamerica." *Expedition* 47, no. 3 (January 1, 2005): 30–36.

Brooke-Hitching, Edward. *The Devil's Atlas: An Explorer's Guide to Heavens, Hells and Afterworlds*. Chronicle Books, 2022.

Burrell, Margaret. "Hell as a Geological Construct." *Florilegium* 24, no. 1 (January 1, 2007): 37–54.

Carrer, Olivier Le. *Atlas of Cursed Places: A Travel Guide to Dangerous and Frightful Destinations*. Hachette UK, 2015.

Cashman, Katharine V., and Shane J. Cronin. "Welcoming a Monster to the World: Myths, Oral Tradition, and Modern Societal Response to Volcanic Disasters." *Journal of Volcanology and Geothermal Research* 176, no. 3 (October 1, 2008): 407–18.

Crisafulli, Chuck, and Kyra Thompson. *Go to Hell: A Heated History of the Underworld*. Simon Spotlight Entertainment, 2005.

Curley, Daniel, and Mike McCarthy. *Rathcroghan: The Guidebook*. 2nd ed. KPW Print Management, 2023.

D'Andria, Francesco. "The Ploutonion of Hierapolis in Light of Recent Research (2013-17)." *Journal of Roman Archaeology* 31 (January 1, 2018): 90–129.

Davis, Gerald J. *The Divine Comedy: The New Translation*, 2021.

Ehrman, Bart D. *Heaven and Hell: A History of the Afterlife*. Simon & Schuster, 2020.

Fitzsimmons, James L. *Death and the Classic Maya Kings*. University of Texas Press, 2009.

Furst, Severine, Tony Hurst, and Bradley Scott. "Variations of the Inferno Crater Lake Cycles, Insights from New Data." Proceedings 36th New Zealand Geothermal Workshop, 2014.

Ihimaera, Witi. *Navigating the Stars: Maori Creation Myths*. Vintage, 2020.

Jennings, Ken. *100 Places to See After You Die: A Travel Guide to the Afterlife*. Scribner, 2023.

Kreiger, Barbara. *The Dead Sea: Myth, History, and Politics*. University Press of New England/Brandeis University Press, 1997.

Kroonenberg, Salomon. *Why Hell Stinks of Sulfur: Mythology and Geology of the Underworld*. Reaktion Books, 2013.

Masse, W. Bruce, Elizabeth Wayland Barber, Luigi Piccardi, and Paul T. Barber. "Exploring the Nature of Myth and Its Role in Science." Geological Society, London, Special Publications 273, no. 1 (January 1, 2007): 9–28.

Mastrolorenzo, G., Pierpaolo Petrone, Mario Pagano, Alberto Incoronato, Peter Baxter, Antonio Canzanella, and Luciano Fattore.

"Herculaneum Victims of Vesuvius in AD 79." *Nature* 410, no. 6830 (April 1, 2001): 769–70.

Pumfrett, Belinda. *Bats About Kasanka*. 4th ed. ARC Limited Zambia, 2021.

Ruzo, Andrés. *The Boiling River: Adventure and Discovery in the Amazon*. Simon & Schuster/TED, 2016.

Veress, Márton, Dénes Lóczy, Zoltán Zentai, Gábor Tóth, and Roland Schläffer. "The Origin of the Bemaraha Tsingy (Madagascar)." *International Journal of Speleology* 37, no. 2 (July 1, 2008): 131–42.

Viramonte, J., and Jaime Incer-Barquero. "Masaya, the 'Mouth of Hell,' Nicaragua: Volcanological Interpretation of the Myths, Legends and Anecdotes." *Journal of Volcanology and Geothermal Research* 176, no. 3 (October 1, 2008): 419–26.

Virgil. *The Aeneid*. Translated by Shadi Bartsch. Random House Publishing Group, 2021.

Virgil. *The Aeneid*. Translated by Robert Fagles. Penguin, 2006.

Vogt, Evon Z., and David Stuart. "Some Notes on Ritual Caves among the Ancient and Modern Maya." In *In the Maw of the Earth Monster*, 155–85. University of Texas Press, 2005.

Waddell, John. *Archaeology and Celtic Myth*. Four Courts Press, 2015.

Wilcox, Christie. *Venomous: How Earth's Deadliest Creatures Mastered Biochemistry*. Scientific American/Farrar, Straus and Giroux, 2016.

Maps and Illustrations Credits

MAPS CREDITS

CENOTES | Ecological and Territorial Planning Program of the State of Yucatán, Secretariat of Sustainable Development; GeoComunes, 2.1.1 Cenotes in the Yucatan Peninsula

HELL'S GATE | (temperature extremes) World Meteorological Organization, World Weather & Climate Extremes Archive; (background map) Fick, S. E., and R. J. Hijmans, 2017. "Worldclim 2: New 1-km spatial resolution climate surfaces for global land areas." *International Journal of Climatology*

LAVA LAKES | Smithsonian Institution Global Volcanism Program

ILLUSTRATIONS CREDITS

Cover, Briony Morrow-Cribbs; 4-5, Richard Roscoe/Stocktrek Images/Alamy Stock Photo; 10, Capture That - Landscapes/Alamy Stock Photo; 14, Richard Cummins/Alamy Stock Photo; 19, Matt Cardy/Getty Images; 22, (detail), Savery, Roelandt Jacobsz. (1576-1639)/Kunsthistorisches Museum, Vienna, Austria/Photo © Fine Art Images/Bridgeman Images; 24, Niklas Ramberg/Dreamstime; 31, Harris Dro/Loop Images/Universal Images Group via Getty Images; 35, HIP/Art Resource, NY; 39, M. Limoncelli,

Archivio Missione Archeologica Italiana a Hierapolis; 42, Francesco Bonino/Adobe Stock; 47, Giuseppe Nappo/Shutterstock; 51, Martin, John (1789-1854) (after)/Laing Art Gallery, Newcastle-upon-Tyne, UK/Tyne & Wear Archives & Museums/Bridgeman Images; 55, Hamish Fenton; 60-1, Remizov/Shutterstock; 64, stenic56/Shutterstock; 67, Thomas Lukassek/ Dreamstime; 71, Eddie Gerald/Getty Images; 72, Steve Estvanik/Shutterstock; 75, mareksaroch.cz/Shutterstock; 79, The History Collection/Alamy Stock Photo; 83, Oman Cave Exploration Team/AFP; 84, AFP via Getty Images; 87, beibaoke/Shutterstock; 90, Alyssand/Dreamstime; 94, WaterFrame_gno/Alamy Stock Photo; 101, Jad Davenport/National Geographic Image Collection; 105, Roberto Destarac Photo/Shutterstock; 106, Images-USA/Alamy Stock Photo; 110, Ian Dagnall Computing/Alamy Stock Photo; 113, studioaccendo/123RF (AI-generated image); 114, Michael Nichols/ National Geographic Image Collection; 116, Martin Bernetti/AFP viaGetty Images; 121, Iwanami Photos/Shutterstock; 123, George Kourounis/ National Geographic Image Collection; 126, Eric Thayer/Bloomberg via Getty Images; 131, Erika Engelhaupt; 134, Jeff Kowalsky/EPA/Shutterstock; 136, Richard Walker Media/Shutterstock; 138-9, Ritu Jethani/Dreamstime; 145, Fabris, Pietro (fl.1768-78)/Private Collection/The Stapleton Collection/ Bridgeman Images; 148, Enrico Della Pietra/Adobe Stock; 151, Massimo Santi/Shutterstock; 156, Desprez, Louis Jean (1743-1804)/Private Collection/Bridgeman Images; 159, Giannis Papanikos/Shutterstock; 160, Tunatura/Shutterstock; 162, Michael Melford/National Geographic Image Collection; 165, Ilan Shacham/Getty Images; 168, Sean Pavone/Shutterstock; 171, Peter Rejcek/USAP Photo Library; 174, John S Lander/LightRocket via Getty Images; 177, Ihlow/ullstein bild via Getty Images; 178, NanoStockk/Getty Images; 183, Marco Brivio/imageBROKER/Shutterstock; 186, Emile LUIDER/REA/Redux; 188, Photopat/Alamy Stock Photo; 192, Vladimir Nardin/Getty Images; 195, George Steinmetz/National

Geographic Image Collection; 199, F. Luise/Getty Images; 200, Carsten Peter/National Geographic Image Collection; 202, Shaun Jeffers/Shutterstock; 207, Carsten Peter/Speleoresearch & Films/National Geographic Image Collection; 208-9, Javier Trueba/MSF/Science Source; 212, Victoria Burt/Alamy Stock Photo; 214, Brian Brake/Science Source; 219, Stephen Alvarez/National Geographic Image Collection; 223, Ashley Cooper pics/ Alamy Stock Photo; 227, Kris Wiktor/Shutterstock; 228, Alan Majchrowicz; 232, George Steinmetz/National Geographic Image Collection; 235, Nico Faramaz/Shutterstock; 238, Andrew Price/Shutterstock; 241, Andrés Ruzo/ National Geographic Image Collection; 245, Tourism Ministry/Xinhua/ Alamy Stock Photo; 248, Westend61/Martin Rietze/Alamy Stock Photo; 251, China Photos/Getty Images; 255, Nick Garbutt/NPL/Alamy Stock Photo; 259, Michael Durham/Minden Pictures (multiple images stitched together); 264, Guenter Standl/laif/Redux; 268-9, Chris Dennis Rosenberg/Getty Images; back cover (LE), Marc Guitard/Getty Images; back cover (CTR), Carsten Peter/Speleoresearch & Films/National Geographic Image Collection; back cover (RT), Chien Lee/Minden Pictures.

Back cover, left to right: Dallol, Ethiopia; Cave of Crystals, Mexico; Tsingy de Bemaraha, Madagascar

Index

About the Author

Erika Engelhaupt is a freelance science journalist, editor, and author. This is her second book published by National Geographic Books. Her first, *Gory Details: Adventures From the Dark Side of Science,* explored some of the strangest real-life science stories she has uncovered in her career. Her writing has appeared in top science magazines, newspapers, and websites, including *National Geographic,* NPR, *Science News, Scientific American,* and *Popular Mechanics.* She holds M.S. degrees in biology and environmental science, and when she's not traveling to hellish destinations, she's home enjoying cooking, eating, and reading (all voraciously). She lives in Washington, D.C., and Knoxville, Tennessee.

"A MUST-READ FOR CURIOUS MINDS, TRIVIA FANS, AND CRIME DRAMA ENTHUSIASTS."

—*Library Journal,* Starred Review

With wicked wit and a dash of morbid curiosity, this provocative narrative from the author of National Geographic's popular Gory Details blog takes us on a fascinating journey through an astonishing new reality where our weirdest and wildest fascinations will be illuminated.

"A delightful collection of stories that will turn you into either the best or worst of dinner guests."

—ED YONG, Pulitzer Prize winner and author of *I Contain Multitudes*

"A creepily readable journey through the world of the gross."

—CARL ZIMMER, author of *She Has Her Mother's Laugh*

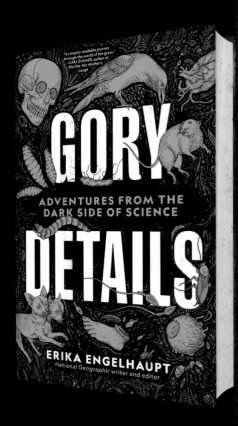

AVAILABLE WHEREVER BOOKS ARE SOLD

  @NatGeoBooks

© 2024 National Geographic Partners, LLC